PORTFOLIO

INSIDE CHANAKYA'S MIND

Radhakrishnan Pillai is a management speaker and strategy consultant with nearly twenty-five years of experience and over 200 articles and papers to his credit. He has a PhD in the *Arthashastra* from the University of Mumbai. Currently the deputy director of the university's leadership science programme, Pillai has taught in many prestigious institutions, including Oxford, Cambridge, Indian Institutes of Technology and Indian Institutes of Management. He has represented India at the World Congress of Philosophy in Athens, the Academy of Management in San Antonio, Texas, and the Indian Philosophical Congress. He received the International Sardar Patel Award in 2009 and the Aavishkar Chanakya Innovation Research Award in 2013 for his contribution to the field of management and industrial development. Pillai is considered one of the top thirty Indian management thinkers globally by Thinkers50. His books include the bestselling *Corporate Chanakya*, *Chanakya in You*, *Chanakya's Seven Secrets of Leadership* (with D. Sivanandhan), *Katha Chanakya* and *Chanakya in Daily Life*. He can be reached at rchanakyapillai@gmail.com.

INSIDE CHANAKYA'S MIND

AANVIKSHIKI AND
THE ART OF THINKING

RADHAKRISHNAN PILLAI

PORTFOLIO
PENGUIN

An imprint of Penguin Random House

PORTFOLIO

USA | Canada | UK | Ireland | Australia
New Zealand | India | South Africa | China | Singapore

Portfolio is part of the Penguin Random House group of companies
whose addresses can be found at global.penguinrandomhouse.com

Published by Penguin Random House India Pvt. Ltd
4th Floor, Capital Tower 1, MG Road,
Gurugram 122 002, Haryana, India

First published in Portfolio by Penguin Random House India 2017

10 9 8 7 6 5 4 3 2

ISBN 9780143427537

Typeset in Adobe Caslon Pro by Manipal Digital Systems, Manipal
Printed at Manipal Technologies Limited India

www.penguin.co.in

MIX
Paper | Supporting
responsible forestry
FSC® C043100

To my children, Aanvikshiki and Arjun, who are curious and always in wonderment.

And to my wife, Surekha, who forces me to think differently as a husband, friend and partner in solving life's problems.

Contents

Contents

1

Introduction to Aanvikshiki

Let me begin with a story.

There was once a child. Whenever he did something wrong, others used to tell him, 'Why are you making so many mistakes? Why can't you understand things well? Can't you think properly?'

When the child went to school, he was brought up in an examination system instead of an education system. When he did not do well in his exams, his parents and teachers used to say, 'Why can't you study properly? Think about what we tell you, otherwise you will not only fail in your exams but also fail in life.'

As a teenager, he fell in love and had his heart broken. His friends told him, 'We had told you not to go after that girl. Why did you not take our advice?'

When he got out of college and worked in various companies, his bosses would say, 'Your effort is important in work—but what matters more is the result. Think about it and you will succeed in your career.'

When he got married, had children and was bestowed with the responsibilities of a householder, the elders in the house would advise him. They said, 'Remember and understand your duties. No one can run away from it. It is part and parcel of life.'

Then came a stage in his life when his children were settled and he was close to retirement. His friend asked him, 'Have you thought about what you are going to do post retirement? Do you have a plan?' He did not.

Finally, he was old and alone. His wife had passed away, his children and grandchildren were busy with their own lives, and he had nothing much to do. He had all the time in the world to look back and ponder over his life.

While reflecting upon every stage of his life—as a child, student, teenager, professional, homemaker, he was constantly advised by others to 'think', to succeed in life and to avoid making mistakes.

He hadn't really got a chance to do an in-depth reflection on the word 'think' at all.

Now, for the first time in his life, he was 'thinking about thinking'.

But was it too late?

All his life, he had been told by others to think. But no one actually taught him 'how to think'.

Does the story tell you something? Does it ring a bell inside your head?

Do you think this story has a connection to your life?

If you really 'think', you will understand that this is a story about all of us. This is a story of every man and woman, every child, every teenager, every professional, the young and the old, the married and the unmarried.

This is the story of you and me.

Strange but true, one can lead one's whole life without thinking.

What a tragedy.

Now let us reverse this story.

Imagine if you were taught how to think from the very beginning, the moment your thinking faculties develop. Instead of loading the child with information, if one taught the child the right methods of thinking—analysis, decision-making, prioritizing, planning, structuring, critical evaluation, logic—things would be different. You would question when questions are required. Accept others' views where it is necessary. Think through all the consequences. Take calculated risks and, without doubt, you will be far more successful. You will be successful not only at the very end, but also at every stage of your life.

In this book, we present something very interesting: Some methods and techniques of thinking, the philosophy of thinking and alternative ways of thinking. This book is simple yet profound. It will lead you to something that will ignite your mind and intellect.

In a sure yet subtle way, it will change your thinking. It will add a new dimension to your views about life in general.

I hope the book becomes a silent killer. It will kill various misassumptions you had in the past. It will kill your ignorance and make you happier. If understood from the right perspective, it will kill your ego. You may die internally once, only to live a full life again.

Most importantly, you will enjoy this journey—it is fun. It will help you discover yourself all over again.

Let us call this process an adventure in thinking.

Let us begin the journey which actually started many centuries ago in India.

Chanakya the Man

Who is Chanakya? To be honest, he was a phenomenon. A legend, a master strategist, a teacher and a philosopher, all rolled into one.

We can hardly find any parallels in world history that come close to him. He could take up any field and become a master of it.

When he studied political science, he became one of the greatest statesmen India has ever produced. When he decided to study military science, he could defeat Alexander on his way to conquer the world. When he decided to dethrone Dhanananda, the strongest king of his time, he made sure he achieved it. He chose an ordinary village child, Chandragupta Maurya, and made him one of the greatest emperors of all time. Gemmology, Ayurveda, espionage, crime, law, punishments—no subject was difficult for him. He was a master of all subjects and became a master of many kings.

He had a kind of magic wand in his hand. Whatever he touched turned into gold.

When he decided to write a book, he made it an all-time bestseller. Kautilya's *Arthashastra*, written in the fourth century BC, sells in large numbers even today. Imagine a book being on a bestseller list for 2400 years and still going strong!

When he decided to teach, he became a teacher whom all teachers could look up to as a role model.

His principles of 'good governance' continue to inspire leaders across the globe. His administrative models are still followed. His accounting systems were flawless.

One even wonders if there ever lived such a man in flesh and blood.

But then, we know for sure that there lived such a man who walked the earth, taught in universities and created leaders, setting standards for others to live up to.

In this book, we get into the mind of this great man.

We will try to dissect his personality. We will decode his intellect, understand his background and his thinking, deliberate over the many ideas he preached and practised, and finally ask ourselves, 'Can I become like Chanakya?'

The answer is yes. Each person has the potential to become the Chanakya of his or her generation.

How to Think

Now, the good news is that thinking can be taught.

Yes, I repeat, thinking can be taught.

People ask us to think, but when it comes to the process, no one talks about it.

Just like the man who was deboarding a flight. The air hostess wished him with a smile, 'Have a nice day, sir.'

The man smiled and replied with a question, 'How?'

The air hostess was stunned. No one had ever asked her such a thing. For the air hostess, it was routine to wish every person—a mechanical action.

In the same manner, when people say, 'Think carefully', 'Think twice, act once', 'Have you thought through about it?'—all these may be just mechanical suggestions.

But if, like the man who surprised the air hostess, we were to step back and ask, 'How does one think?', hardly anyone will be able tell us the process.

But Chanakya was different. When he said something, he meant it. What he achieved in his life was due to a well-thought-out plan. And, therefore, he could also teach others how to think.

This process of thinking is called *aanvikshiki*.

I am sure that most of you reading this book are hearing the word for the first time. We will talk about aanvikshiki in detail in this book. But before that, let us explore one more aspect of Chanakya—the amazing book that he wrote, the *Arthashastra*.

I would urge you all to read the *Arthashastra* in detail at some point in your lives. It is a book that will change your thinking—one of the greatest books on thinking, written by one of the greatest thinkers from India.

Yes, the *Arthashastra* can change your thinking, because it teaches you how to think—like a leader.

Kautilya's *Arthashastra*

Kautilya is another name for Chanakya.

Artha means 'wealth', in a broad sense, while *shastra* means 'scripture'.

So, Kautilya's *Arthashastra*, a book written by Chanakya, is considered to be a scripture on wealth.

Once a student and now a teacher of Kautilya's *Arthashastra*, I have been amazed by this book again and again. Every time I read this book, it makes we wonder, 'How can one man write on so many subjects in one single book?' Yes, there are nearly 180 topics that Chanakya has written about in this book.

That is why it is called a scripture—something which contains ancient and eternal knowledge.

During my own research, I found that there were many Arthashastras before Chanakya wrote his own. The word 'arthashastra' was not invented or coined by Chanakya— it did exist before him. We find the earliest references to 'arthashastra' in the Rig Veda, the oldest Indian text.

The *Arthashastra* has been dealt with at length in the Mahabharata as well. Bhishma, the great grandsire, is considered as one of the great exponents and teachers of Chanakya's work.

The *Arthashastra* is also considered as the science of politics, economics, warfare, and a text that relates to governance, leadership and strategy. It is also a book on law, foreign policy, international relations and how to rule a territory.

The Process of Writing the *Arthashastra*

Chanakya is clear in his thinking.

He has a methodology and a process while he writes the *Arthashastra*. Unlike most of us, he declares, at the very beginning of his composition, how he wrote the book.

The opening sutra in the opening chapter starts by telling the readers what the background was when he wrote the book:

This single treatise on the science of politics has been prepared mostly by bringing together the teaching of as many treatises on the science of politics as have been composed by ancient teachers for the acquisition and protection of the earth (1.1.1)

Chanakya openly declares that his work is a collection of many works. There were many ancient teachers who taught the Arthashastra before Chanakya. He had studied all the ancient books himself. Before one creates knowledge, one ought to thoroughly study the existing knowledge available.

The world of knowledge is continuously evolving. It always grows. The existing knowledge is expanded with the help of every generation. Each generation adds its experiences and wisdom and contributes to the field of knowledge.

Thus, the first step in knowledge creation is research, and it is this research that leads to development.

Chanakya had done research and studied the existing knowledge of his field and subject—the Arthashastras. He studied them in detail, made notes and compared the same with his experiences before writing his own treatise.

So his creation of the *Arthashastra* is based on others' work—and yet it is original. Originality does not come because one starts from zero. Originality comes from going into the depths of any subject and uncovering new insights. Those insights are original creations, much like Chanakya's work. Throughout the *Arthashastra* that he wrote, one can find quotes and thoughts of other teachers. Yet, he took them and interpreted them in a different manner. This interpretation and presentation is what is original about his book.

The same principle applies to every field of knowledge. Take physics, for example. Einstein's Theory of Relativity is considered an original contribution to the field of physics. The formula $E=mc^2$ has redefined various aspects. It has become a guiding principle for students, researchers of physics across the globe.

Yet, we know that physics as a subject existed long before Einstein. We also know that as time passes by, there will be more scientists who will do research in the subject and invent new formulas and findings. In spite of all the additions and deletions that may happen in the area of physics, Einstein will continue to be remembered as a great scientist. His contribution will be remembered forever, and his findings will provide solutions to many future researchers.

Future generations will look upon the work of Einstein with respect and, in some way or other, his theories will become a reference point.

The same goes for Chanakya's work. Even though Chanakya did not invent the field of Arthashastra, he studied the subject in depth, analysed it, discussed it with experts, even criticized it and critically evaluated the ideas. Finally, he formed his own opinions on the subject.

The writings in Kautilya's *Arthashastra* are rich, containing 6000 sutras. Each sutra is profound and rigorous, and makes you think. It brings together the various experiences of masters, experts and teachers of the Arthashastra.

The Purpose of Writing the *Arthashastra*

Why was the *Arthashastra* written by Kautilya?

As Kautilya says—for the acquisition and protection of the earth.

What does that mean?

First of all, the work was written primarily for leaders, the kings of his generation, and specifically for Chandragupta Maurya—his able student.

Chanakya says:

This science has been composed by him (Kautilya), who in resentment quickly regenerated the science and the weapons and the earth that was under the control of the Nanda kings. (15.1.73)

Chanakya refers to himself over here. That he in anger and frustration had dethroned the last king of the Nanda dynasty (Dhanananda) and regenerated—meaning, recreated—the whole art of good governance (the science of politics) through this work, the *Arthashastra*.

Chanakya also concludes the *Arthashastra* by once again asserting the purpose of his writing.

Seeing the manifold errors of the writers of commentaries on scientific treatises, Vishnugupta himself composed the sutras as well as the bhasya. (End note)

Now here is the interesting observation.

While studying the previous works of other great scholars of the Arthashastra, Chanakya observed many errors in the past writings. This is but natural. When you read something written by someone else at some other point of time, there will surely be some errors. It is the responsibility of every generation to correct them. You cannot change the works of the past. But, you can avoid making the same errors in future works.

For example, when a book is written, in the flow of the text the author may miss many finer points. There could be spelling mistakes, grammatical errors and so on.

It is the work of editors and proofreaders to correct the mistakes and give a good structure to the text. So, when the book comes out, it is ready to go to the readers.

Now, here is the catch. In the perfect book too there is a scope for updating it. There will still be some mistakes. In spite of one's best efforts, there is always a chance of human error. Even the best proofreader and editor might miss things.

So, what is the solution?

When you find the mistake, make a note of it and correct it in the next edition or reprint—it's as simple as that.

So does Chanakya take into account some errors and improve on them in his own work. Chanakya does that improvement in the *Arthashastra* too—and he admits it.

He knew that future generations were likely to find faults in his own work. Then it is the freedom of the new generation of authors to correct and improve his work.

There were many Arthashastras written before Chanakya. And there were many more composed after him. But Kautilya's *Arthashastra* still stands strong. It has survived the test of time, and has become a classic.

Salutations to this great master who learnt from the other masters. He teaches us never to condemn those before us, but to improve upon their teachings.

Aanvikshiki

Welcome to this new word.

Welcome to a new science.

Welcome to a new subject.

Welcome to a new way of thinking.

Welcome to a completely new world altogether.

Aanvikshiki—I call it the science of strategic thinking. Some people call it critical thinking. R.P. Kangle, one of the profound scholars of the *Arthashastra*, called it philosophy. Aanvikshiki is also logical thinking, scientific thinking, inquiry and research.

Swami Tejomayananda (the head of the Chinmaya Mission) in his classic composition *Mana-shodham* calls aanvikshiki a *bhrama vidya*—it is self-knowledge, enlightenment and a path leading to self-realization, moksha, nirvana and mukti.

Aanvikshiki is a Sanskrit word with various meanings. One has the freedom to interpret, reinterpret and even discover new meanings of the same word.

The only rule is that the meaning of the word should help us elevate our thinking. As long as this is taken care of, one can give new dimensions and perspectives, depending on our understanding.

Let us look at the word 'dharma'. It means ethics, morale, righteousness, duty, responsibility and many more. One can even give new meanings to it.

However, let us look at the Sanskrit meaning of 'dharma' to understand the word better. Dharma comes from the root word *dhir*, meaning 'to hold'. So *dharayati iti dharma* means dharma is 'that which holds'.

Nothing can exist without something. It is the very essence of a thing, the very nature and property of an object. So, what is the dharma of fire? It is heat and light. Remove heat and light from fire, it will no more be fire at all. Remove sweetness from sugar and it is no more sugar.

Dharma is the very base and foundation of any object. Everything exists based on dharma, including the natural laws.

In a similar way, let us understand what aanvikshiki stands for.

Let us go to the root word in Sanskrit, which most scholars regard as the most ancient, scientific and perfect language of the world. It is also called the mother of all languages.

Aanvikshiki is the combination of two words—*anu* and *ikshiki*. Anu means 'atom', the smallest part of anything. Ikshiki means 'a person who wants to know', an inquirer, a thinker, a researcher, an examiner or a logician.

Therefore, aanvikshiki is the process of enquiring and right thinking, or the science of thinking. Now as a reader you can also offer your own interpretation after studying and practising aanvikshiki yourself.

Aanvikshiki was one of the names of Draupadi in the Mahabharata. She was a brilliant woman who had studied the science of thinking.

We find various mentions of aanvikshiki in other scriptures like the Shrimad Bhagawat, the Ramayana and even in the Upanishads. So, even though for us aanvikshiki is a new word, it was quite popular in ancient times.

Aanvikshiki in Kautilya's *Arthashastra*

The first and opening chapter of Kautilya's *Arthashastra* talks about aanvikshiki and its importance.

The *prathama prakarna* (first section), named 'Vidyasamuddesha' (enumeration of the sciences), starts with the chapter 'Aanvikshiki Sthapana' (establishing the necessity of thinking).

Chanakya wants his students to study aanvikshiki as their first subject. Imagine teaching thinking as the first subject in our education system. What an amazing way to begin.

If at all we could teach our children in schools to think, inquire, ask, question, apply logic and then establish and have their own individual conclusions, what a brilliant generation would come out of our schools, colleges and universities.

What we follow instead is herd mentality. Just do what others are doing. Go to school—study, get a degree, secure a job and education is over. This kind of system rarely helps to get the best out of an individual. From a data-driven education system, we need to move into a process of investigation and inquiry.

Let us teach our children to think and wonder, to imagine, to construct, to create, to dream, to visualize and to build their own future in a unique manner.

This is what Chanakya did in his education system. He wanted his students to be leaders. And the first quality of leadership is to think correctly and clearly. From such clarity comes good decision-making capacity. And sound decisions have an impact on everyone.

Now let us get started and study the first chapter of the *Arthashastra*, which is about the science of thinking.

Book one, section one—'Aanvikshiki Sthapana'

Right thinking (aanvikshiki), the three Vedas (trai), economics (vaarta) and the science of politics (dandaniti)— these are the sciences (vidya) (1)

'The three Vedas, economics and the science of politics are the only sciences,' say the followers of Manu. (2) 'For, aanvikshiki is only a special branch of the Vedic lore.' (3)

'Economics and the science of politics are the only sciences,' say the followers of Brihaspati. (4) 'For, the Vedic lore is only a cloak for one conversant with the ways of the world.' (5)

'The science of politics is the only science,' say the followers of Usanas. (6) 'For, with it are bound up undertakings connected with all the sciences.' (7)

'Four, indeed, is the number of the sciences,' says Kautilya. (8)

Since with their help one can learn what is spiritually good and material well-being, therefore, the sciences (vidyas) are so called. (9)

Samkhya, yoga and lokayata—these constitute aanvikshiki. (10) Investigating, by means of reasoning, what is spiritual good and evil in the Vedic lore, material gain and loss in economics, good policy and bad policy in the science of politics, as well as the relative strength and weakness of these three sciences, aanvikshiki confers benefits on the people, keeps the mind steady in adversity and prosperity and brings about proficiency in thought, speech and action. (11)

Aanvikshiki is always thought of as the lamp of all sciences, as the means of all actions and as the support of all laws and duties. (12)

Note: The above English translation of the original Sanskrit version of the chapter on aanvikshiki is taken from *Kautilya Arthashastra* by R.P. Kangle (a Sanskrit teacher at the University of Mumbai), published by Motilal Banarsidass.

Kangle refers to aanvikshiki as a philosophy in his English translation.

Detailed Explanation of Each Verse in the Chapter on Aanvikshiki

Right thinking (aanvikshiki), the three Vedas (trai), economics (vaarta) and the science of politics (dandaniti)— these are the sciences (vidya). (1)

There are four vidyas (subjects) that a student has to learn.

These four types of knowledge are fundamental to becoming a good leader:

1. Aanvikshiki—the science of thinking (philosophical thinking)
2. Trai—the three Vedas (Rig, Sama, Yajur) in the later generations. Atharva Veda was added as the fourth Veda.
3. Vaarta—economics (agriculture, cattle-rearing and trade). These were the three prime economic activities during that time.

4. Dandaniti—political science (the science of punishment and good governance)

In any education system, the design of the programme is very important.

So, when a school, college or university designs a course, the syllabus is decided first. This is the first step a teacher takes.

The syllabus is the foundation of the course. Based on the syllabus set by the teachers, the whole teaching system is decided. They will then recommend textbooks, reading material and other resources. Even expert teachers will be invited to teach those subjects that are in the syllabus.

Thus, we find that Chanakya in the very opening stanza gives the course outline to everyone. The student is the prime focus when Chanakya is writing the *Arthashastra*. So, before any student joins the course, he or she will want to know what they are going to learn.

Chanakya, therefore, begins with explaining what he is going to teach.

Aanvikshiki, trai, vaarta and dandaniti—these four vidyas together constitute the knowledge of the king.

Throughout this book, we will be focusing on aanvikshiki, the first knowledge of a king.

But then a leader also has to know trai, the Vedas. The Vedas contain the knowledge of the universe. It is not written by one person. These are the mantras that were revealed to great men of realization, called rishis. It was Veda Vyasa, also known as Adi Guru, on whose birthday we celebrate Guru Poornima, who compiled these Vedas.

The knowledge of the Vedas spans various subjects, both worldly and metaphysical.

One who does not make his kingdom strong economically is not a good leader. Therefore, Chanakya included vaarta as a subject in economics. A leader should not be a trader, but he should encourage trade. He needs to create an environment where business can flourish, ample tax is collected and used for the welfare of the people.

Finally, dandaniti—the art and science of politics. It is also called the method of ruling and leading a place. Unfortunately, today, politics is seen as a negative word, despite the fact that political wisdom gives the ability to rule and lead well.

'The three Vedas, economics and the science of politics are the only sciences,' say the followers of Manu. (2) 'For, aanvikshiki is only a special branch of the Vedic lore.' (3)

We saw earlier how Chanakya takes references from the previous acharyas and teachers of the Arthashastra. Here we see him referring to Manu (a great teacher and of a school of the Arthashastra). Chanakya brings in the view of another great master. Manu had said that there are only three sciences (vidyas), not four as given by Chanakya.

Why does Manu say so? Is it because aanvikshiki, which is treated as a separate subject by Chanakya, is already included in the three Vedas (trai), so is it not required to be treated as a separate subject at all?

'Economics and the science of politics are the only sciences,' say the followers of Brihaspati. (4) 'For, the Vedic lore is only a cloak for one conversant with the ways of the world.' (5)

Again, Chanakya brings in another contrarian view of Brihaspati, who is the teacher of the gods. Brihaspati does not accept four or three vidyas, but only two of them—economics and the science of politics. For it is observed that Vedic tradition is only a cover for the worldly wise. They only believe in the world of things and beings—not the other worldly.

'The science of politics is the only science,' say the followers of Usanas. (6) 'For, with it are bound up undertakings connected with all the sciences.' (7)

This is a different view from Usanas (a teacher of the Arthashastra). They only believe in political wisdom. The other three, according to them, are dependent on or connected to politics.

The politicians are the lawmakers, and laws govern everything. So ultimately, politicians control the system. Hence one belief shown here is that 'he who understands politics, understands everything'.

But finally, Chanakya has his own conclusion to make:

'Four, indeed, is the number of the sciences,' says Kautilya. (8)

Chanakya reiterates what he originally said, that vidya includes all the four sciences—aanvikshiki, trai, vaarta and dandaniti.

Chanakya gives aanvikshiki the importance of a separate and important subject. He feels it should not be mixed up with the other three. Aanvikshiki should be treated as an area of specialization, not generalization.

Even though the other teachers refer to aanvikshiki, it is not in the way Chanakya has done—to treat it as something more than just another idea, and make it the crown jewel among all subjects.

According to him, all the four vidyas are important. Yet, aanvikshiki, the right way of thinking, should be given its due place in the field of knowledge.

Chanakya continues to explain why all four sciences are important.

> Since with their help one can learn what is spiritually good and material well-being, therefore the sciences (vidyas) are so called. (9)

When all the four science are learnt, one can learn worldly knowledge and spiritual knowledge. To succeed in life, both are important. One cannot just be materially rich and spiritually poor. And one should not be just spiritually successful but a worldly failure.

Indian wisdom teaches us to be both spiritually and materially developed.

Now comes the most important part: What is aanvikshiki, according to Chanakya?

> Samkhya, yoga and lokayata—these constitute Aanvikshiki. (10)

Nowhere else in Indian literature, before Chanakya, do we find such importance given to aanvikshiki, that too, with such a detailed analysis of the theme and idea.

Aanvikshiki is a philosophy, which includes three other philosophies.

Sankhya: It is one of the oldest philosophies attributed to the great Kapil Muni. It is mentioned in the second chapter of the Bhagavadgita. It also comes from the word *samkhya*, meaning 'numbers'.

Yoga: It is now a very popular method of exercise to keep oneself physically fit. However, yoga is not just at the physical level but also at the level of the mind, the intellectual and spiritual level. Sage Patanjali wrote the yoga sutras and designed the *ashtanga* style. Yoga comes from the root word *yuj* which means 'to join or connect'.

Lokayata: This is another school of thought, and is often referred to as materialistic philosophy. However, in our culture, even materialistic thought is respected. So the philosophy which teaches one to be materially successful is also important.

Hence we can interpret aanvikshiki as a way of thinking which includes numbers, the right connection to divine and material success. A person who thinks simultaneously in numbers, divine connections as well as material success is one who practises aanvikshiki. Therefore, aanvikshiki is a very practical way of thinking.

How to Practise Aanvikshiki

Investigating, by means of reasoning, what is spiritual good and evil in the Vedic lore, material gain and loss in economics, good policy and bad policy in the science of politics, as well as the relative strength and weakness of these three sciences. (11)

One needs to investigate with reason. It is important to think logically and systematically.

So this kind of thinking is not just an emotional outburst. It is a well-thought-out process.

Practising aanvikshiki requires one to consider three things:

1. Good and evil (according to Vedic tradition—trai)
2. Material gain or loss (according to economics—vaarta)
3. Good policy and bad policy (according to the science of politics—dandaniti)

Additionally, it includes the consideration of the relative strength and weakness of the three sciences mentioned (trai, vaarta and dandaniti).

So, while thinking about something, we need to carefully measure its pros and cons. Is it spiritually good? Will it give any material gain? Is it the right policy decision?

Thus, when we consider various dimensions, we will be able to take the right and correct decision, weighing all the consequences.

What Is the Benefit of Aanvikshiki?

Aanvikshiki confers benefits on the people, keeps the mind steady in adversity and prosperity and brings about proficiency in thought, speech and action. (11)

The best part of aanvikshiki is that it is not just a selfish way of thinking. It does not consider only personal gain. It confers benefits to everybody. It keeps the mind steady in all situations. Keeping ourselves calm and composed is the reward that aanvikshiki brings to a person. Be it adversity or prosperity, loss or gain, good or bad times, sickness or health—in all circumstances, we find that the practice of aanvikshiki helps maintain the balance of the mind.

It brings about proficiency in

1. Thought—it gives clear thinking (clairvoyance)
2. Speech—verbal communication
3. Action—there is perfection in all activities

And finally,

> Aanvikshiki is ever thought of as the lamp of all sciences,
> as the means of all actions and as the support of all laws
> and duties. (12)

This is the ultimate praise Chanakya accords to aanvikshiki.

Aanvikshiki is the guiding principle for everything in life. It is like a lamp guiding us in darkness. When we travel to an unknown region, we require a road map, a guide and some assistance. That support is aanvikshiki.

It is the guiding lamp (*pradeep*) of all sciences. It is the means and method of taking the right action. It is the supporter of all laws and duties.

Therefore, whatever we do using aanvikshiki as our foundation will be perfectly planned and executed, and results are guaranteed.

And all this will be ethical, legal, moral and spiritual.

It will be completely *dharmic*, abiding laws and duties. In the following chapters we will see how aanvikshiki can be practised. Let's begin our journey.

2

Types of Thinking

'As the thoughts, so the man,' said Swami Chinmayananda, the great spiritual teacher.

Can we choose our thoughts? Is it possible to choose the way we think? Well, in order to choose we require options first.

Suppose there is only one school in a village. Is there an option to choose? Now if there are many schools in the village, one can exercise choice.

Similarly, can we choose our thoughts and the way we think?

Yes, as long as we have different ways of thinking, we can make our choice.

Our thoughts come randomly in our minds. The mind is a flow of thoughts. We require little effort to create thoughts. They just happen. In fact, it requires a lot of effort to stop our thoughts. If thoughts go unchecked, it may be dangerous and even lead to a loss of mental balance.

The process of controlling one's thoughts and calming one's mind is called meditation. Once our mind is under control, we can do wonders. Mind power can create anything in this world, for a person whose mind is fully under control is a superman.

There are various types of thinking. And we can choose from the choices available. When we choose the right kind of thinking, we can create wonders. The wrong type of thinking can destroy us completely.

This choosing of the right kind of thinking is also aanvikshiki.

There are two broad types of thinking that most people are aware of—positive thinking and negative thinking. We are usually told by others to practise positive thinking. But in reality, positive thinking is not enough. We need to have practical thinking. Between optimistic thinking (positive thinking) and pessimistic thinking (negative thinking), there is something called realistic thinking (practical thinking). Therefore, let us not be either optimistic or pessimistic—let us be realistic.

As we proceed further, Chanakya gives us an indication of the various types of thinking he practised and preached. You don't have to choose one and stick to it— different types of thinking can be used together.

1. Both-side Thinking

One of the reasons why Chanakya was considered brilliant was because he used to look at both sides of a coin. Only looking at one dimension cannot really give us the full picture.

Many so-called positive thinkers do not like to think of failures. They live in an imaginary utopian world, where everything seems to be good. There is nothing wrong in that. It is important to dream and think big.

Dr Abdul Kalam, former president of India, inspired a whole generation by asking them to dream. He gave wings of fire to our imagination. If one does not dream, one will never be able to create a new world. We should be able to lift ourselves from where we are to where we should be. For that to happen, we need to think big and be positive.

However, relying only on positive thinking can be dangerous too. When reality hits, it can result in depression. Such a person will tell himself, 'I had a dream and the world is the problem. It does not allow me to fulfil the dream.' These people then become so negative that one wonders what happened to all the energy they displayed while they started on their journey to achieve their dreams.

Dreaming is the perfect start to any project. But it is important to factor in ground realities in our thinking as we undertake the journey, so that we do not turn back when we encounter any hurdles on the road. We just solve the problem and keep walking towards our destination.

When the river flows towards the ocean, which is its destination, there are many challenges it faces. Yet, the river keeps flowing. If a rock blocks its path, the river will simply flow around it and create a new path. The river will never lose its focus. And finally, it will merge and become one with the ocean. Our dreams are fulfilled in a similar way.

We need to learn from Chanakya; we need to look at both sides as we start on our journey.

The *Arthashastra* opens with an interesting prayer:

'Om Namah Shukra Brihaspati Abhyam'
(Salutations to Shukra and Brihaspati)

There is a hidden secret in this prayer. When Chanakya starts to write the *Arthashastra*, as we have previously seen, he refers to all the former teachers. But, he starts by saluting two great gurus, namely Shukra and Brihaspati.

Shukra was an acharya, the guru of the Asuras. A brilliant master, he was a teacher and is known for his work *Sukra Niti*, which offers strategies.

Brihaspati, on the other hand, was the guru of the Devtas. He is also considered to be the planet Jupiter. Brihaspati too was a great teacher of political science.

Now, imagine this—the Asuras and the Devtas are at war, and both are guided by their respective teachers. It is similar to a football match, and both teams have coaches who train and guide the players. A brilliant student would like to learn from both coaches. Why take the side of one team and one teacher? This is where Chanakya offers salutations to both teachers.

Another interesting point is that he offers salutations to Shukracharya first and then Brihaspati. The idea is to look at the counter view first and then towards the good side.

There is a Sanskrit saying, *'Durjana prathama vandana, sajjana dada nantaram'*.

Which means the *durgan* (the wicked) should be saluted first and then the *sajjan* (the good). Here we are not supporting the wicked or wickedness, but learning from both.

When you look at both sides of an issue, your thinking evolves. Knowledge of the other viewpoint only enriches your thinking. Good people will anyway give you good advice, but the wicked will show you the loopholes in your thoughts. You can consider both arguments before making your move.

Always take the opinion of both sides—the truth may lie in between.

2. Alternative Thinking

There can be one solution to many problems. There can be many solutions to one problem.

For example, if there are many problems in an organization, Chanakya says there is one solution to all the problems—the leadership. If we get the right leader, the problem will most likely be solved.

Say there is a financial crisis. There could be various solutions to manage that financial problem: work hard and make the money, take a loan, borrow from a friend, sell some of your assets and so on.

This is called alternative thinking. The problem and the solution are both in our minds. Train the mind in the right kind of thinking, and you will always succeed, no matter what the problem.

That is why we need to develop a 'solution-focused' mindset rather than one that is 'problem-focused'. Either you become a solution to every problem, or you turn out to be the problem.

There are various methods of alternative thinking detailed by Chanakya in the *Arthashastra*. But the most famous four-step process is called '*Sama, Dana, Bheda, Danda*'. Even though this four-step process was primarily used in military strategy, Chanakya uses it in other fields like foreign policy, international relations, crime detection, law and order, and punishments.

Let us try and understand these four aspects first.

Sama (discussion): The first step is to never start a war. Most problems can be resolved amicably. If there is mutual respect between two people, just a mature discussion is all it takes to achieve a win-win situation.

Dana (giving gifts): This is an interesting method. It is human nature to love gifts. So, when we gift something to a person, we can win them over and achieve our objectives. Look at what mutual benefit can be achieved. Most misunderstand this as bribing.

Bheda (division): This is for people who are unfriendly. Divide and rule. Try to analyse the problem and understand who may agree with your point of view in order to get the desired results. When direct methods do not work, try this indirect method that could.

Danda (force): Some people and situations are absolutely unchangeable or unrelenting. When nothing works, we need to use force. This is the final step used to achieve our objective. Therefore, war is the last and final alternative used by Chanakya to win the game.

Now, the sequence of the four steps may not be in the same order. It can be changed according to the requirement and demand of the situation.

If a person is attacking you with a weapon, do not go for sama as the first step. You may not survive to have a discussion. One may need to use danda directly to protect oneself from the attacker.

When giving a gift works, why go for war? In international relations, we find heads of states visiting each other, holding discussions (sama) and also paying their respects to each other by hosting programmes and giving gifts (dana). A peaceful solution is always in everybody's best interests.

Chanakya says:

He should win over those of them who are friendly with conciliation (sama) and gifts (dana), those hostile through dissensions (bheda) and force (danda). (11.1.3)

Essentially, there are two types of people—friendly and unfriendly. For those who are friendly, sama and dana work. For those who are unfriendly, bheda and danda need to be used.

Even though all the four steps are known, we need to develop our thinking skills to decide what works for which situation and which person. This is where the wisdom and maturity of the person becomes essential. Thus, alternative thinking is about choosing the right option according to the demands of the situation.

Countries and governments have been seen using these alternatives for their benefit.

They have ambassadors who are primarily trained in sama. They would discuss issues concerning both states and build relations. They are essentially meant to maintain a balance of power and ensure mutual respect.

The trade and business community of a nation would, on the other hand, focus on dana. Business interactions and the economy are sustained by these groups with the support of the government. Exchange of goods and services ensures mutual benefit.

While friendly nations practise these two options, the unfriendly ones use the other two. There are spies and espionage systems in every country. They use bheda as a tool. They would be planted in the enemy country, and if required, they can even create internal disharmony. Let the enemy bleed through the divide and rule policy.

Finally, we have the military, which uses danda. The armed forces are trained for combat. The air force, the war ships and the infantry, along with their machines and weapons, wage direct wars. There will be destruction, but sometimes to ensure peace, wars are needed.

Choose between the given alternatives to achieve your goals and results.

3. Leadership Thinking

Chanakya trained kings in how to think. What kind of leadership thinking did he want his students to develop? There are many dimensions of thinking that he wanted his students to develop to become a good leader.

However, if we narrow it down to one important aspect of the thought processes of a leader, then this sutra stands out among all of them:

> In the happiness of the subjects lies the benefit of the king and in what is beneficial to the subjects is his own benefit.
> What is dear to himself is not beneficial to the king, but what is dear to the subjects is beneficial to him. (1.19.34)

A king does not have any personal agenda. Or rather, he should not.

In other words, those who do not have any personal agenda and work selflessly go on to become great leaders.

Leaders work for the benefit of others. However, it is easier said than done. But that is how thinking and attitude was meant to be developed as far as Chanakya was concerned.

In the happiness of the subjects is the happiness of the king—what does this mean? It is easy to understand if you start thinking like a parent. In the case of a parent, in the happiness of the children lies the happiness of the parent. They would sacrifice everything to make sure that the child does well in life.

Even if they have not eaten, the parents will ensure that the children are well fed. Even if they are not highly educated, they will do anything to ensure the children get the best schooling they can.

When the children succeed, the parents feel like it is their victory too. This is the depth of the parents' feelings towards their children.

Similarly, the leader has to align his thoughts with those of the citizens he is serving. Leaders cannot be selfish or use the subject for personal benefit alone. All great leaders have worked relentlessly for the uplift of their people. There is no other agenda at all.

By accepting what he or she wants does not guarantee happiness for someone. Just supplying what is demanded is not good parenting or able leadership. There are two Sanskrit words *sukha* and *hita*. Sukha is happiness, but hita is well-being.

Sometimes a person's well-being may take precedence over their happiness—just as when a doctor may recommend a bitter dose of medicine, which is unlikely to make the patient happy. But the doctor will insist on the medicine for the well-being of the patient.

Similarly, a child may cry while going to school. But the parents force the children to go and get educated anyway. The children may not feel happy, but the parents know it is for their well-being.

In the same way, leaders have to take tough decisions for the well-being of the people. Although it may not appear to be a happy feeling in the beginning, it will make us happy in the long run.

At times we see that the government raises the taxes, which citizens usually protest against. But if the government is not selfish and is only using the higher taxes for the benefit of the people, then they will soon see the benefits.

The taxes will be used for the health and education of the citizens, better roads and transportation and other facilities. Soon, people will begin to see the benefits of raising taxes.

I would like to share a story with you to illustrate this point. Once, a person was taken to the gallows because he had committed a murder. When asked about his last wish, he said he wanted to meet his mother. When the crying mother came to see her son, he told her, 'You are responsible for my death.' The mother was shocked.

He recollected a childhood incident and said, 'Mother, remember the day I came home after stealing a chocolate from a friend, and you never corrected me? I took it for granted that everything I do will be accepted by you.'

He continued, 'When I started doing bigger crimes, then too, you just supported me. Today I have committed a murder and am going to meet death soon. I just wish you had stopped me when I stole the chocolate. I would have lived longer.'

Therefore, leadership thinking is not just about making people happy and accepting whatever the popular feeling is. A king should listen to every person who comes to meet him, and consider every idea deeply. If required, the king should also consult some experts. Then what is right must be done.

A leader should set a standard where a standard does not exist. A leader is also a creator.

He should sometimes think out of the box. He should also inspire his people to work towards a higher purpose, goal or vision.

But whatever the leader does is for the benefit of the people. There are times when the leader has to make personal sacrifices in order to make people happy.

Once a leader was asked, 'You work so much for others, but what about your family?'

With a smile, he said, 'All those people are also my family.'

For an individual, a family may be a limited to his wife, parents and children, along with a few relatives.

But for a leader, the whole country or organization is his family. He cannot think of only himself; he has to think about the well-being of each and every person.

Kautilya's *Arthashastra* goes one step further. It says the king has to take care of not only human beings but also animals, birds, plants, minerals, water bodies and all else that is part of his kingdom.

Thus, according to Chanakya, leadership thinking is an all-inclusive thinking. It encompasses the living and the non-living.

Finally the leader is responsible for anything and everything that is part of his kingdom. This thinking leads to effective governance and good administration.

4. Creative Thinking

One very important aspect of Chanakya's way of thinking is about being innovative and creative. When we read the *Arthashastra*, we find how creative he was. He was not a stereotypical thinker. Chanakya loved to experiment with ideas. In everything he did, he used creativity.

Let us see an example of this:

Chanakya said: 'The time for catching elephants is summer.' (2.31.8)

This sutra comes in the chapter titled 'Superintendent of Elephants'. In this part of the *Arthashastra*, we find Chanakya giving a lot of tips to the head of the department of elephants. During those days, elephants were considered as important assets of the army and the nation. To have a strong force of elephants was a need and necessity. Like in business it is important to have lot of customers, so too, having many elephants in the department was a key to success.

Chanakya gave creative tips on how to catch elephants. This means he studied the behaviour of elephants.

Chanakya knew that creativity works only if we are at the right place at the right time. If we miss the right time, we may not get it again.

There are two concepts in creative execution: right time and right timing. For example, if a children's movie has to be released, we need to take both these aspects into consideration.

The 'right time' for releasing a children's movie is during the vacation season and school holidays.

The 'right timing' is when the children will want to go to see the movie. So an early-morning show at 6 a.m. at a theatre nearby will not work. The children or the parents who will accompany them will never go to watch a movie at 6 a.m.

So even though the movie may be released during school holidays (right time), an afternoon or evening show (right timing) is equally essential for the success of the film.

In India, a movie featuring a superstar will mostly do well. The release of the movie on a holiday—say, Diwali, Dussehra, Eid or Christmas—makes a huge difference. The collection of movie ticket sales is always high on weekends.

A similar psychology applies in say the FMCG (fast-moving consumer goods) segment. The highest sales of groceries and home products will be on a Saturday, a Sunday or a holiday; the shopping malls will be filled with customers then, while on the other days there is hardly any footfall.

Market research experts who give companies advice on how to sell their wares are always at work trying to understand customer behaviour patterns about what is the right time or timing to sell products and services.

However, according to Chanakya, creativity does not mean destruction. Some people believe in disruptive creativity. It means creating by destroying something. You never look good by making someone look bad.

'Only if I destroy the other person will I succeed. My software product will sell only if I destroy the other person who creates a software product. If my company has to do well, I need to destroy the competitor.'

This kind of approach in creative thinking was not taught by Chanakya.

Even while catching elephants, he was considerate. He knew the limits and did not want to destroy the ecosystem in which elephants live.

Chanakya said:

A twenty-year-old should be caught. A cub, an elephant with small tusks, one without tusks, one diseased, a female elephant with young and a suckling female elephant are not to be caught. (2.31.9–10)

Only a twenty-year-old elephant should be caught. It has grown up and is independent. It is young and strong. It is healthy and can work.

The main purpose of an elephant is either in the army to fight against the enemies. Or, it could be do some heavy work like carrying loads and goods. For this, any elephant cannot suffice. It requires a strong and dynamic elephant. The twenty-year-old elephant is the right fit.

If someone has to be recruited in an armed force, there is are age restrictions. Recruitment ads clearly specify the age group.

Creativity is about what to do. Creativity is also about what not to do.

So, as Chanakya is indicating when and what type of elephants are to be caught, he also mentions which elephants are not to be caught.

A cub elephant, one with small tusks, is not meant to be caught.

It is interesting to note the psychology of elephants that Chanakya uses here. Unlike tigers or eagles, who live alone, elephants operate in groups. Therefore, catching a young elephant is not good. The cub elephant and the teenaged elephants require their family and friends. Taking such a young elephant away from the group is not encouraged.

The same goes for a mother elephant, as she has to feed her small ones. Also, an old or diseased elephant should not be caught. The biggest medicine for any disease is 'love'. When we are sick, we require our loved ones around us, apart from the doctor's medication.

So, while creativity should be our focus, let us not be inhuman. Let us not be destructive. Let us not go against nature. Instead, let us all tune in to nature and work in accordance with its laws.

In today's scenario, environment management is a major challenge. We are faced with difficult questions of harming nature, as well as other species.

We all have to work with nature and its creation.

So let us be creative in a natural manner.

Let nature be our guide and our best teacher of creativity.

5. Lateral Thinking

Thinking out of the box is often required to tackle a situation and get the desired results.

But sometimes, you have to check whether the box even exists. You might just have been imagining that you were stuck in a box, while the fact was that you were always free.

So another type of thinking shown by Chanakya is lateral thinking.

All things remaining the same, a few people succeed, while others fail.

For example, I have personally worked as a trainer and consultant with two companies that manufacture cement. One company is super profitable and is confident that it can overcome any financial turmoil for the next twenty years. The second company, on the other hand, has not been able to pay salaries to its employees, is going through absolute financial instability and is on the verge of being sold off.

In the first company, all the stakeholders are happy, while in the other company, employees are insecure and have lost all confidence. What could be the reason?

They work in the same country, they have the same customers, the government policies are the same and the environment and ecosystems they operate in are the same. Yet there is a huge difference between the two of them.

This is primarily because of two reasons—leadership and strategy.

The leadership of the first company is always focused on the long term. They have a vision and a mission. They believe in research and development, invest in the right people, take calculated risks and have the best industry experts as their guides, mentors and consultants.

The second company's management is focused on the short term. They want quick profits, do not take time to think before sacking employees, are impulsive while taking decisions and believe that all they are doing is right. The leaders consider profit as the only parameter of success.

Good leaders need to have good strategy as well. Through careful, well-planned strategies, we develop lateral thinking. Chanakya was a master in teaching strategy and lateral thinking.

To make this process easy, he also developed the game of chess.

Game of Chess

In the olden days, the game was called *chaturanga*, meaning four parts of the army (*chatur* means four and *anga* means parts).

This board game based on military strategy was played by kings as a pastime. However, through the game, they were able to gain insights into warfare and develop strategic acumen.

From chaturanga, it became *shatrang* as it went to the Arab countries in the Middle East. And finally, in the European and Western world, it got the name 'chess'.

The war game has four principal components.

CHESS stands for:

- C: Chariots
- H: Horses
- E: Elephants
- SS: Soldiers

There is an interesting chapter in the *Arthashastra* which teaches us how to plan a war based on these four components: 'Modes of Fighting of the Infantry, the Cavalry, the Chariots and Elephants' (book ten, chapter five, section 157).

This is a brilliant chapter on the various permutations and combinations that can be used by the king to defeat his enemies.

Note that in the modern game of chess, both sides have the same number of soldiers, elephants, horses and other pawns. It is not that the winner had more horses or elephants. Both sides are also subject to the same rules and restrictions. The different pieces can only move in certain ways, and this applies equally to both sides.

So what makes one a winner and the other a loser? The way they use their resources. The moves and the strategy used make all the difference. This is where lateral thinking comes in.

Businessmen and management gurus often talk about optimal utilization of resources. So how you use these resources available at your end makes you a winner.

Chanakya said:

> Foot-soldiers (should be) in the wings, horses on the flanks,
> elephants in the rear, chariots in front, or a reversal of this
> (may be made) in accordance with enemy's array. (10.5.38).

Every person has to be positioned in a certain manner. The arrangement of the troops is structured so that everyone knows their roles and responsibilities, and does their duty well.

Look into any office or factory. There is an arrangement for where people sit and what they do.

The moment you enter, there is a reception area, where you are attended to and welcomed. Then there are various people and departments who sit inside the office—accounts, sales, IT and so on.

Then there is the place where the leader sits. There will also be a manufacturing area, a canteen and so on. In a similar manner, it is important to plan how we position ourselves in our life and workplaces.

But what is critical in the game of chess, Chanakya says, is that we should change our strategy to account for the enemy's array.

To develop lateral thinking, we need to understand the moves made by the enemy. At times, you flow with the moves of the enemy. At other times, you move to surprise the enemy.

If we are able to understand the modus operandi of the other person, then it is easy to achieve victory. Therefore, the teachings of Chanakya are about studying the other person.

First we need to understand our own thinking. Next we need to understand the thinking of others. When we combine both, success in anything we take up is guaranteed.

6. Spiritual Thinking

Chanakya was known for his multidisciplinary thinking. He could think in various dimensions. He made India the wealthiest country of his time.

He wrote the book that is considered a scripture on wealth, 'artha-shastra'. He understood finances like no other person. He made new economic models and theories. The creation of wealth and wealthy kingdoms was his expertise. The treasuries of the kingdom that he guided were not just full, but overflowing.

In spite of all this material wealth he created, one thing that we should not forget is that Chanakya was a deeply spiritual person. He was a very enlightened person. He created riches outside, but what really mattered was inside.

For Chanakya, knowledge was wealth. Knowledge was his greatest weapon, knowledge was his greatest asset, knowledge was his strength and knowledge was his greatest power.

He said, 'If I have knowledge, I can create many emperors.'

Where did he get this conviction? It came from the depth of his spirituality. He had an absolute conviction in himself and God Almighty. The spiritual base and foundations that he had were strong and deep-rooted.

Therefore, one more type of thinking that Chanakya wanted leaders to develop was spiritual thinking.

Dharma is the core word that is discussed in all our Indian scriptures. Making the leader a *dharmic raja* or a *rajarishi* was his highest vision. In the *Arthashastra*, the word 'dharma' appears 150 times.

Dharma denotes various concepts and ideas—it is morality, ethics, spirituality, duty and responsibility, among others. Chanakya speaks at length on *raja dharma*, the duties and responsibilities of a king.

As we are ending this chapter, we will take a closer look at spiritual thinking.

Chanakya said:

He should enjoy sensual pleasures without contravening his spiritual good and material well-being; he should not deprive himself of pleasures. (1.7.3)

There is a common misconception about spirituality—that it is meant for old and useless people, and that you become spiritual only when you have nothing left to do in life.

Another misconception is that spirituality is for the other world, to gain benefits after we die and go to some place called heaven.

In reality, it is the other way around. The really spiritual people are always active and dynamic. They are action-oriented.

The spiritual energy in them gives them the strength to do better than the ordinary. With a foundation of spirituality, even the ordinary will become extraordinary.

Yet another misconception is that spirituality is related to poverty. In the above sutra, Chanakya says to enjoy material wealth along with spirituality, and also that everyone should fulfil their material desires in a spiritual manner.

There are four aspects one should be aware of in life. These are called the *purusharthas* in our Vedic culture.

1. Dharma: spiritual good
2. Artha: material well-being
3. Kama: sensual or worldly desires
4. Moksha: enlightenment

Chanakya says the first three have to be balanced in our lives, that is, 'dharma', 'artha' and 'kama'. So one should surely enjoy material success and fulfil all worldly desires. But this has to be done on the foundations of spirituality.

Once we understand that, moksha or spiritual enlightenment will follow in due course.

People have misconceived notions about moksha—that it is something that happens suddenly, it is something that changes you externally and gives you some kind of halo around your head.

Spirituality is a state of awareness. It is a state of being with oneself.

In the Bhagavadgita, Krishna says an enlightened person is a *sthitha-prajna*. 'Sthitha' means established. 'Prajna' means knowledge and wisdom. Therefore, a sthitha-prajna is a person who is established in knowledge and wisdom.

Chanakya wants every person to be wise. However, that is a very high state. For beginners and average people like us, it is advised to balance dharma, artha and kama.

So if you run a company or an organization, you should create a lot of wealth and money (artha) and fulfil all desires (kama), but it should be based on spirituality (dharma).

There is nothing wrong in being ambitious and creating wealth. One can desire to become the richest person in the world. Only make sure that the wealth is created in an ethical manner.

Becoming wealthy or rich is very easy. Even gangsters and dons are rich. But they are not the role models we should give to our next generation.

Becoming rich the spiritual way seems difficult, but that is the right method. Making money through shortcuts seems easy, but shortcuts are usually the longest ways to true success.

A rich businessman said it nicely: 'Wealth that is created quickly also vanishes quickly. Wealth that is created slowly and steadily stays longer and becomes permanent.'

Hence, Chanakya trains his students in spiritual thinking.

Spiritual thinking also means to be in tune with the laws of nature. The law of the universe is all around us. If we can understand these spiritual principles that govern everything around us, we will never fail in anything.

Finally, Chanakya had said, 'He should not deprive himself of pleasures.'

Who said spiritual thinking means torturing oneself? Do not deprive yourself of pleasures—enjoy life. Never suppress your desires. Because if we do that, then one day, they will erupt like a volcano and destroy everything around us.

Fulfilling our desires in the right method is the solution.

We should know our limits—*maryada*. A person who is self-disciplined can enjoy life to its fullest without any harm.

Thus, among all the types of thinking brought out by Chanakya, the highest form is spiritual thinking. But only spiritual thinking without worldly thinking is also not good. Balance everything in life. A life thus lived is fulfilling and without any regrets.

Live life king-size. But the heart should also be large in size, to accommodate one and all.

That is the reason why, apart from being the greatest political thinker, Chanakya was also known as one of the greatest 'practical philosophers' that our country ever produced.

3

The Different Models of Thinking

What is thinking?

It is not just sitting idle and imagining things. Thinking is a very structured process. It is very scientific and logical. Aanvikshiki, the right way of thinking, is very systematic in nature. Throughout the *Arthashastra*, Chanakya gives us different models of thinking.

One day, Chandragupta Maurya was sitting alone. He was thinking of various issues that he had to face as a leader. In a complex situation, he often could not decide what to do or how to move forward. Whenever Chandragupta was stuck in such a situation, he usually took the help of his guru, Chanakya. This time too as was his habit, he immediately called his attendants and asked them to arrange a visit to meet Chanakya. His guru was living in an ashram in the outskirts of the kingdom at that time.

As soon as he reached the ashram, Chandragupta rushed to his teacher's room. But he was surprised to find that his guru was missing. He immediately asked the other ashram inmates, 'Where is Guruji?' They replied, 'He has been away for a couple of days now. He did not tell us where he is going or when he will come back.'

Chandragupta did not know what to do. He felt helpless without his guru. Chandragupta waited for Chanakya. He even sent his team out to find his guru, so that he could meet him. But once Chanakya decided to go unnoticed, it was difficult even for the gods to find him.

Looking for Chanakya or waiting for him seemed to be a futile exercise. Left with no choice, Chandragupta called his other ministers and advisers, and tackled the situation in hand. The problem was resolved and the kingdom was relieved.

After a long time, Chanakya came back to his ashram. He came to the palace to meet Chandragupta. Seeing the guru in front of him, Chandragupta was thrilled. Rushing to him and touching his feet, he said, 'Acharya, please never do that again. Don't go away like this. Who will guide me in solving the complex problems of our country?'

Chanakya gave a naughty smile, as if his going away was by design.

'Did the problem get solved?' he asked.

With hesitation, the student said, 'Yes, we managed somehow.'

'Remember, Chandragupta,' the master advised, 'never depend on anyone to solve your problems. Yes, you should take advice and guidance. But if none is available, take a call on your own. You have to take decisions.' After a pause, he continued, 'After all, you are a leader. Leadership is all about taking decisions in complex situations.'

Chandragupta had a question. 'But how do I take the right decisions?'

There was a sparkle in the teacher's eyes, as if to indicate he was coming to the point. 'That is why I had taught you aanvikshiki, the science of thinking, which will help you take the right decisions, with or without guidance.'

Thus there are various thinking models that Chanakya had taught Chandragupta, so that when the situation demands it, he can use them and take the right decisions from the choices available.

What are these thinking models? There are ready-made prototypes already created and perfected for others to duplicate them. Throughout this chapter, we will be trying to understand some of the different models that Chanakya had created.

We will pick up two types of models that will help us understand how structured thinking was done:

1. Leadership models
2. Administrative models

The leadership models include Chanakya's vision of an ideal leader. It was that of 'rajarishi', a philosopher king. In the section of administrative models, we will explore Chanakya's vision of the administrative set-up of a nation; it is worth a study. Bureaucracy and good administration is the backbone of a nation. The administrative models are available for us to apply and benefit from.

Therefore, these two aspects of thinking models will open our minds. After having studied and understood these thinking models, we will be able to make it a permanent part of our thinking minds. These models will come in useful—in crises as well as in good times. Although we may take some time to understand these thinking models initially, once they become a part of our minds, we have easy access to them.

It is like studying the alphabet and multiplication tables in our schools. The alphabet and multiplication tables are thinking models. They are concepts that are taught to us by repetition. In the initial days, students find it a bit difficult to understand these concepts. But once it becomes a part of our minds, we can recall them and use them anytime and anywhere.

When a book has to be read, the alphabet will come to our rescue. When a calculation has to be done, the multiplication tables will help us. These are the benefits we get once we have understood and developed thinking models.

1. Leadership Models

Rajarishi—Chanakya's ideal leader

Chanakya had developed a model of an ideal king. This concept of an ideal leader is called 'rajarishi'.

Rajarishi is a combination of two words, 'raja' and 'rishi'. Raja means 'a king or a leader' and rishi means 'a sage or a thinker'. For Chanakya, an ideal ruler was like a 'philosopher king'. This kind of a king is a spiritual thinker. His thoughts are deep and profound.

There is a chapter in Kautilya's *Arthashastra* (book one, chapter seven) that describes a rajarishi in detail and also what qualities one needs to develop in order to become a rajarishi.

How does one become a rajarishi? This leadership model of thinking is shown in the following sutra by Chanakya:

By casting out the group of six enemies, he should acquire control over the senses, cultivate his intellect by association with elders, keep a watchful eye by means of spies, bring about security and well-being by (energetic) activity, maintain the observances of their special duties (by the subjects) by carrying out his own duties, acquire discipline by receiving instruction in the sciences (different fields of knowledge), attain popularity by association with what is of material advantage and maintain proper behavior by doing what is beneficial. (1.7.1)

Let us look at these qualities in detail.

By casting out the group of six enemies: There are enemies outside and there are enemies inside a kingdom. The internal enemies are more dangerous than the external ones. And if one is able to manage the internal enemies, it should be easy to control the external enemies.

So who are the internal enemies? Chanakya says that they are the negative qualities that lie within us. Once we are able to get rid of them, no one can defeat us externally.

Our primary enemies are a group of six: lust, anger, greed, pride, arrogance and foolhardiness.

Overindulgence in anything is lust. Losing our temper is anger. Wanting more than what is required is greed. Overpossessiveness is pride. One who gives too much importance to oneself is arrogant. And one who is reckless is foolhardy.

Removing the above vices is a mental model of developing leadership qualities. Be aware of these negative qualities within us. Slowly and steadily, with awareness, try and weed them out to awaken the leader in you.

By acquiring control over one's senses: We have five senses—sound, touch, sight, taste and smell. We understand the outside world using these five senses through our sense organs—our ears, skin, eyes, tongue and nose.

By controlling these five sense organs, we will restrict the entry of unwanted things into us. For example, by controlling the tongue, we can resist eating junk food and maintain our health. If we avoid using our mobile phones and gadgets too much, we will automatically avoid being addicted to gadgets.

By cultivating one's intellect by association with elders: There is a formula Chanakya offers to develop the intellect—by association with elders. The word 'elder' does not mean just senior by age but also one who is senior by experience and wisdom.

So, a leader will become a better leader if he or she associates with wise people. We find that, in Indian history, kings were surrounded by wise men. By using the knowledge and wisdom of others, one can automatically develop and cultivate one's intellect.

Therefore, one of the ways to become intelligent is to associate with those who are more intelligent than us.

By keeping a watchful eye, using spies: Spies are informers. Information is the key to success, according to Chanakya.

The leader has to process whatever information is gathered, come to the right conclusion and take the right decision. This framework and model of thinking helps him or her to be effective. Therefore, Chanakya advises us to be alert and very well informed through a network of spies. The spying and espionage system created by Chanakya is still considered to be one of the best in the world.

By bringing about security and well-being through (energetic) activity: The primary duty of a leader is to ensure the security and the well-being of his people. But how does one achieve this? By energetic activity, according to Chanakya.

Whatever activity is carried out in a kingdom should be full of energy. Enthusiasm (*utsah*) is the key to success in any activity. Enthusiasm is also very contagious. People become enthusiastic if they are exposed to such a vibrant environment.

So whatever activities are started by the leader should be full of drive, rigour and passion. Thus, by working with high levels of energy, the safety and security of the people are achieved.

By maintaining the observance of special duties (by the subjects): Now comes a very interesting dimension of leadership thinking.

The leader should make sure that others do their duties properly. There are duties (dharma) and there are special duties (*swadharma*). There are general duties that everyone has to follow—reaching one's workplace on time, finishing one's work with perfection, being honest in one's profession and so on.

However, people should not forget their special and important duties—for example, the responsibility of taking care of children and elders at home. The king, as a leader, has to ensure that the subjects maintain and observe these special duties, in order to keep the society together.

In India, taking care of one's parents or senior members of the house, is now an essential duty of every family. If not, it is legally punishable.

By carrying out his own duties: Chanakya gives leaders a warning here. A leader can order others to fulfil their duties. But what about himself or herself?

The leader should not shun his duties. This is the first step towards successful leadership. He or she has to walk the talk—show leadership by example. He or she has to be a role model for others to follow. Demonstration is the best way of telling others what to do.

A leader's thinking should include 'If I do my work properly, I automatically gain the power to tell others to follow their duties properly'.

By acquiring discipline by receiving instruction in the sciences (different fields of knowledge): A leader should be a self-disciplined person. Self-discipline leads to success. And how can one achieve self-discipline?

One of the ways of doing this is by following the instructions of the experts. For instance, if you want to be healthy and fit, you may have a health coach. The yoga instructor and the nutritionist will give you a routine to follow. By following their instructions, in a self-disciplined manner, one achieves good health.

Leaders are supposed to receive instructions in various subjects. When we gather knowledge in different disciplines, various possibilities become open to us. This is yet another key to success.

By attaining popularity by association with what is of material advantage: A leader has to ensure economic prosperity. One who works towards material prosperity automatically becomes popular. Therefore, Chanakya suggests that the right way to attain popularity is to ensure development and wealth creation.

So, the leader has to be associated with the kind of projects that will bring richness to everyone. Entrepreneurs are wealth creators, job creators as well as happiness creators. By creating such a positive ecosystem, the leader automatically gains popularity.

By maintaining proper behaviour by doing what is beneficial: One has to ensure proper behaviour at all times. A leader is the face of the organization, the institute or the country he or she represents. If a leader does not behave properly, it impacts the image not only of himself or herself, but the whole body that he or she represents. Therefore, leaders have to be fully aware of their behaviour—in front of others as well as when they are alone. As the popular saying goes, 'The character of a person is judged by how they act not only in front of others, but also when they are in the dark all alone.'

2. Administrative Models

There is a new subject called 'design thinking', in which we need to mentally design the models we want to create. When the mental design is ready, it is easy to implement. Many of us implement models without a mental design. But a framework is required to be created before we start any work.

According to Chanakya, these mental frameworks (referred to as 'thinking models' here) need to be ready structurally in our minds. Then you can gather these pieces and construct the picture that you want, just like a jigsaw puzzle.

Something similar applies to administration also. When Chanakya created a leader like Chandragupta Maurya, he also understood that Chandragupta the king required an effective administrative system. Without strong and efficient administrative and secretarial support, a leader cannot be effective.

Efficient leadership includes an efficient administration. To administer effectively is the secret of good leadership.

There are many administrative models in the *Arthashastra*. In this chapter, we will look at the three key principles that create good administrators:

a. The selection of administrators
b. Testing the integrity of administrators
c. Supervision—key to administrative success

We will also look into the suggestions that Chanakya has offered on how to focus on these three aspects. Note: 'Good administration leads to good governance—the key to making people happy.'

A. The selection of administrators

It is said that the selection of your life partner is the most important decision you will ever take, and that your happiness or unhappiness in life will totally depend on that one decision.

This thought is not just relevant in married life, but also in your role as a leader. The decision of who is going to be your life partner has to be thought through. Similarly, who your administrators are going to be must be carefully decided.

There are many chapters in the *Arthashastra* that are dedicated to ministers and superintendents of various departments of the government. During his days, Chanakya created about eighteen departments that were efficiently run during Chandragupta's rule.

The models are worth a detailed study for modern-day administrators in the government, the bureaucracy, private companies and even the armed forces. The administration process created by Chanakya may have become outdated with time, but the principles of administration never change.

The principles that were relevant 2400 years ago are still relevant today. With the usage of technology in administration, we can create more efficient systems. But how do we select a good administrator?

Chanakya says:

From the capacity for doing work is the ability of a person judged. And in accordance with their ability, by suitably distributing ranks among ministers and assigning place, time and work (to them), he should appoint these ministers. (1.8.28–29)

The king is dependent on his government machinery, which runs the kingdom on a daily basis. The day-to-day affairs of a country are handled by the administrators. These administrators (ministers) have to be selected carefully. So what is the criterion for such a selection? According to Chanakya, the ability of an administrator is judged by his capacity to do work.

There are administrators who are lazy and focus only on the paperwork. When new work comes to them, they do not like to take it up. They do not see new projects as opportunities. These administrators are obsessed with red tape. Anyone who is enthusiastic about a new idea or project will get discouraged when working with such people.

Now reverse the scenario. When someone comes up with a new plan, if the administrator says, 'Very good idea, I think we should try this out. I will give you all the support that you require. If there are rigid rules for the project, I will show you a way out. If you need any help with the paperwork, I am here. I feel this project will be of help to society. Together let us make it happen,' the person is motivated to do his or her best.

A person who is good at a job will be given more work. This is the law of nature. Such people also create new work. They are enthusiastic and thus energize those around them. Such administrators are leaders in themselves.

If there are people who can manage multiple projects, select them as administrators, advises Chanakya. According to their ability, they should be given the required rank and designation. Some people can only handle one project at a time. Some can manage about ten projects at a time. There are some rare administrators (like rare gems) who can handle a hundred projects simultaneously.

A good leader will know the capacity of each of his team members and will give the work accordingly. If a person who is capable of doing one project at a time is given a hundred projects, that administrator will get burned out. Stressed, he will not even complete one project properly.

Now what if the person who is capable of handling hundred projects is given only one project? He too will get frustrated in a different manner. The person thinks, 'I am wasting my time here. The work assigned to me can be finished in no time. It is a no-brainer for me. The remaining time I am sitting idle. Give me more work.'

So the right person should be given the right amount of work.

The leader has to ensure such people are also given the right designations (ranks). If a person is capable of running a full organization, do not make him or her a vice president. Make that person a CEO or a business unit head. They will feel empowered and work enthusiastically.

The place of their posting is also equally important. High-performing government officials are underutilized if posted in some remote areas. It is almost like a punishment for them.

When these high-performing officials are posted in state capitals or national capitals, directly reporting to a chief minister or the prime minister, they can work wonders.

They clear files at super speed, get into execution mode immediately and consistently deliver results.

These administrators also have to be given time frames for projects. Goal-setting exercises are helpful. When leaders and administrators work in 'mission mode', they can achieve amazing possibilities that can be achieved.

As Patanjali, the great yoga rishi, said:

When you are inspired by some great purpose, some extraordinary project, all your thoughts break their bonds: Your mind transcends limitations, your consciousness expands in every direction and you find yourself in a new, great and wonderful world. Dormant forces, faculties and talents become alive, and you discover yourself to be a greater person by far than you ever dreamed yourself to be.

When we work with deadlines, everything just falls into place. Delays stand out as a waste of time. Leaders, therefore, work on timelines.

Time is important in administration. Timing is equally important.

Administrators who know the value of time never waste a single moment. They are punctual, they do not delay matters, they take decisions promptly.

Our time in this world is limited. We all have to find a purpose in our lives. When that purpose becomes our priority, we become creators of a legacy, giants who have great ideals to achieve and who create institutions that last.

As Swami Chinmayananda said, 'A single ideal can transform a listless soul into a towering leader among men.'

So while looking out for an 'ideal administrator', find people with purpose. If not, you should give them a purpose.

Looking at all these above qualities, the administrator should be appointed to the right job or rank at the right time and place. This will ensure happiness to the leader as well as his administrators.

B. Testing the integrity of administrators

Corruption is directly linked to leadership and administrators.

If the administration is corrupted, there are bound to be leakages in the system. There will be financial problems. And the whole society will have to bear the consequences of this failure.

Financial corruption is only one among the many forms of corruption. There is corruption at the moral level, corruption in the form of supporting the wrong person and, the most dangerous one of all, corruption in the form of wanting to be known as a good person. Therefore, an administrator has to have the highest level of integrity.

One may appoint the administrator based on his ability to work. That is a good start. But don't be happy with the best performer. Here comes a warning from Chanakya: Even the most capable administrator could be a biggest danger to the country.

The administrator might show an impressive performance but later, once he is accepted in the system, he or she might slowly turn overconfident and begin to believe that they are above reproach and can now do whatever they want.

The report of a renowned consulting firm showed that 86 per cent of internal frauds in any organization are perpetrated by people in senior management positions. Now that is something to be wary of.

Therefore Chanakya warns:

After appointing ministers (and administrators) to ordinary offices in consultation with the councillors and chaplain, he should test their integrity by means of secret tests. (1.10.1)

An administrator or a minister is appointed first in ordinary offices—that is, given minor tasks. This is done in order to check if the person is appropriate for the job or not. A leader should never appoint an administrator on his whims and fancies. It is a scientific process of recruitment. Like what human resources (HR) departments do in most companies.

The appointment is done in consultation with the councillors and chaplain. A leader requires advice and advisers at every point in decision-making. The *raja purohit* will also check the horoscope of the person to be appointed in order to determine his qualities and whether he is compatible with the thinking of the king and his kingdom. After the administrator is appointed, there are some secret tests to be conducted to confirm the integrity of the person.

Most organizations have some sort of probationary period for new employees. This is a time of experimentation. The new person is part of the organization, yet not fully. Some companies even refer to such appointees as interns, management trainees or temporary employees.

During this period, the boss or the leader keeps a close watch on the new employee. This period of observation can last from three months to even a few years. When someone fit for the organization is found, he or she is given a permanent post or designation.

What are the kinds of tests that have to be given to such temporary administrators?

There are four tests of integrity: the test of loyalty, the test of material gain, the test of lust and the test of fear. These are conducted without the knowledge of the person who is being tested. Section six of chapter ten of book one of the *Arthashastra*—'Ascertainment of the Integrity of Ministers by Means of Secret Tests'— is dedicated to this topic. For those who are in the job of recruiting people in organizations, especially for senior management positions, this section of the *Arthashastra* is worth a detailed study.

Let us now look at the four tests.

1. The test of loyalty: During the probationary period, the person is tested on his loyalty. A colleague of his (sent by the system) says something along the lines of 'The king is bad, and if we can destroy him, both of us can rise to power immediately.' If the person agrees, it means he is not loyal. However, if he rejects such an offer, he has passed the test of loyalty.

2. The test of material gain: Next, another person a spy in disguise is sent. He will try to bribe the person. 'You are in such a big organization in such a high post. Kindly do this work for me and you will get this benefit in return.' If the person takes the bribe, it is understood that he is a potential threat to the organization. If he disagrees immediately, he can be trusted with financial transactions.

3. The test of lust: Sexual harassment at the workplace is a serious concern to the leaders. And an administrator is a powerful person, who may misuse his power in return for sexual favours. Chanakya would send someone to offer such a favour. If the person agrees, then he has failed the test of lust. If not, he can be trusted in this aspect.

4. The test of fear: This is the most interesting one—the test of whether a person fears death. How would he behave when death approaches? The real integrity of a person is decided here. A situation is created where the newly appointed administrator is caught and threatened with death. Then he is told, 'The only way to escape death is to kill the king. We have a plan. Join us.' If he agrees, he is disloyal. If he disagrees, it is guaranteed that even in the worst situation, he will not go against the king or his country.

Passing all these tests, the appointed administrator moves from a temporary position to a permanent one. The person becomes part of the king's core team. Now that his loyalty is proved, he can be given higher responsibilities.

He will be loyal and honest till death.

But hold on . . .

Chanakya would keep his thinking hat on. He will never take any person or situation at any point for granted. So here comes another thinking model to ensure good administrators administer well.

C. Supervision—key to administrative success

'The mind is a flow of thoughts,' said Swami Chinmayananda.

Nothing is constant. But the mind is the most inconstant thing we can ever imagine. A person is what his thoughts are. Thoughts continuously change. So our mind is also continuously changing.

Chanakya was a master psychologist. He understood the human mind. Depending on the mental capability of the person, he would assign different tasks to them. We do not work with people. We work with people's minds. Once we understand this formula, nothing is hidden from us.

The mind can trap you, but can also liberate you. Krishna in the Bhagavadgita also indicates this: 'The mind is your friend and your enemy.'

If we know how to use our minds we can succeed in anything that we do. Life is nothing but a mental game. Understand the mind and enjoy the game.

Many believe that Chanakya would not trust anyone. In reality, Chanakya did not trust their minds. He knew that the human mind is inconstant. That is why he made sure he kept an eye even on the king and his ministers.

Chanakya in his administrative set-up had quite a few checks and balances. He had watchdogs to accomplish this. He had spies and he had spies who spied on the spies.

The advice to a leader to set up a good administrative system was:

The leader should constantly hold an inspection of their works, men being inconstant in their minds. For, men being of a nature similar to that of horses, change when employed in works. Therefore, he should be cognizant of the worker, the office, the place, the time, the work to be done, the outlay and the profit of these undertakings. (2.9.2-4)

This is a very profound piece of advice, given by a man who was a psychologist, mind reader and taskmaster.

Let us break it down and try to understand this advice in detail.

Constantly hold an inspection of their work: The word 'constant' is very important here. If regular inspection and reviews are not carried out, the people working under you may slip up.

Supervision is an important aspect of good administration. One type of supervision is regular standard supervision. These are produced by standard operating procedures (SOPs). Most organizations also have management information systems (MISs).

But there is another type of inspection—surprise checks. This is like when a teacher suddenly announces a test when no one in the class expects it. Good students will pass the test, because they are ready at any given point of time. The others will become alert and vigilant and will come prepared for the next time.

Men being inconstant in their minds: People are always inconstant in their minds. As we keep doing our work, there are chances of losing the focus. We may lose direction and our purpose. The leader's main job is to give direction and make sure his men are on the right track.

The journey may be long and trying, but if we have a purpose, it keeps us going on in the right direction. (Note that the administrator also requires direction from time to time.)

It is like driving a car—from time to time, it is important to look at maps to check if we're on the right road. The dashboard will also indicate the correct speed and indicates the fuel requirement.

Men, being of a nature similar to that of horses, change when employed: Horses are strong animals. They are royal in nature. So, when they are put to work, they resist. A good horse trainer knows that it will take a little while to tame a wild horse. But once tamed, the horse's power becomes the biggest asset in getting work done.

Chanakya here compares the mind to horses. When told to do something, everyone initially resists. But then, if the mind is tamed and brought under control, it can do wonders.

Therefore, one should be cognizant of the worker, the office, the place, the time, the work to be done, the outlay: Leaders should be aware of the workers and administrators. They should keep an eye on the office, the place of work, the timing of work, the work to be completed and also the expenditure.

Factories keep a track of when workers come and go. If salaries are paid on a daily basis, it becomes even more important. Today, we have biometric attendance systems that obviate the need for human intervention.

Additionally, organizations set up goals and key result areas (KRAs) for employees to focus on.

Profit of these undertakings: Chanakya was not a businessman, but he meant business. He would always focus on the return on investment (ROI) as far as his people and administrators were concerned. In a way, he was focused on financial returns.

A good administrator understands that the economic viability of a project is essential to measure its success. Financial success is an important indicator of success.

A leader should understand financial excellence (FE) along with people excellence.

In this chapter we saw many different mental models of thinking.

If thinking can be structured and made into models and frameworks like these, it will create a systematic base of knowledge. It becomes organized.

Knowledge is important. Organized knowledge is even more important—it is the next step to success. So organize your thinking. The aanvikshiki way. The Chanakya way.

4

The Seven Dimensions of Thinking

As we grow, our thinking changes. It evolves with time. We think differently than how we used to think ten years ago. As life progresses and we age, we gather experiences. These experiences change our thinking and also our personality.

As children, we are more imaginative thinkers. But as we grow, we start thinking logically. We rely more on our intellect. We ask more questions. Why? How? What? Where? When?—and many more such questions cross our minds. If we find one answer, we automatically go to the next question on the list.

It is this type of inquiry that forms the foundation of intellectual growth. One question leads to another, and another. The quest for knowledge keeps growing. In such a phase of inquiry, if a person finds a suitable guide, teacher and mentor, then it is very happy stage of life. If not, life becomes a struggle.

Chanakya was a guru and a teacher par excellence. With experience, he knew what kind of questions would be asked by students at what stage of their studies.

A good teacher knows when the student is ready and when to reveal the answers. When the time comes, the teacher will give the appropriate questions appropriate replies, in an appropriate manner.

Usually, when students enrol in an educational institute or a course, they are not really sure what to expect from the course. Most students join a course either due to the decision taken by their parents or going by some information given by their friends. This is common in our generation. When a student joins a college and is asked, 'Why did you choose this course?' there are only a few who can answer this question with conviction.

This situation was true even in the olden days. Chanakya knew the mindset of each of his students and why they had joined the university where he was a teacher. He also knew that there were certain maturing points in a student's life. When they reach these maturing points, they ask mature questions. During those moments, Chanakya was ever ready to give mature answers to such mature students.

There are three defining moments in a student's life. The first is the moment when he or she joins a course. The second is when the course or the educational programme is completed. This is usually the convocation ceremony. The third defining moment is when he or she understands what the importance of the education that has been acquired is.

Chanakya was not really interested in the start or the end of the course. Those for him were just calendar dates for the record. He was more interested in the stage when students asked the important questions about the course, the syllabus and the implication of the knowledge acquired.

One day, a student was sitting all by himself. He was a prince and had been studying *rajaniti*, political science, under the guidance of his guru, Chanakya. One of the primary textbooks for this course was the *Arthashastra*, which Chanakya himself had authored under the pen name of Kautilya. Suddenly a question rose in his mind, 'Why am I doing all this? Why am I studying the *Arthashastra*? What am I supposed to do after studying rajaniti?'

Chanakya knew these questions had set the student thinking in the right direction. The student was ready with the right questions.

'Acharya,' the student began, 'what is the purpose of this gurukul and the text I am studying?'

The guru replied, 'You are studying the science of politics, which is called rajaniti or *raja vidya*. This is the knowledge of the kings and for the kings. The *Arthashastra*, the book on rajaniti, tells you how to succeed in the field of politics and leadership.'

Another question came into the mind of the student. 'Why am I doing this course?'

Chanakya smiled, remembering the day the student had come to his gurukul. His father, the king of a small neighbouring kingdom, had come to request Chanakya to teach his son the way of good leadership. That was many years ago.

He had arrived as a small boy with wonder in his eyes. Today, he was a young teenager almost ready to take up any challenge.

'Your father was keen that you get a good education. And since you were born to a royal family, everyone expects you to be a born leader. So, you are here to learn the ways of leadership and good governance.'

The prince thought for a moment and inquired, 'So, Acharya, if I am going to be a king, tell me, what is a king supposed to do?'

Giving him a strong purpose in life, Chanakya said, 'A king or a leader is supposed to lead the kingdom. Rule well. Take care of his citizens as his own children. Bring economic and material prosperity. But also ensure there is spiritual progress along with it. The overall welfare of everyone in the country is his foremost duty.'

Thinking deeper, the student's questions continued. 'If a king is supposed to lead a kingdom, tell me, what does a kingdom consist of and how does one lead it? Is there a system?'

Chanakya was happy that he could teach the prince the crux of leading a kingdom. 'Yes, there is a way.' After a pause, he continued, 'It is called the *saptanga* of a kingdom.'

The curious student never stopped questioning. 'What is saptanga?'

And the acharya's answer was deep and profound. He continued to explain in detail.

Saptanga—The Seven Parts of a Kingdom

'Saptanga means *sapta* (seven) and *anga* (parts).'

Chanakya continued, 'These seven parts of a kingdom are also called prakritis. Prakriti means 'nature'. So these seven parts of the kingdom are natural parts of the state or nation.'

'Once he understands these seven parts of a kingdom properly, a king or a leader's job is to keep them together and intact. He has to make sure these seven parts are taken care of properly. Keeping them united, fit and running, the kingdom becomes an ideal kingdom. It becomes like a well-oiled machinery that keeps operating to make everyone happy . . .'

The curious prince then asked, 'What are these seven parts of a kingdom?'

Chanakya laid out his model for a kingdom:

> Swami, amatya, janapada, durga, kosha, danda, mitra—iti prakritaya. (6.1.1)
>
> (The king, the minister, the country (people), the fortified city, the treasury, the army and the ally—are the constituent elements [of the kingdom])

Then with profound insight, the acharya declared, 'Understand these seven parts of a kingdom in detail. And then you will be able to understand your role as a leader. Study the *Arthashastra* well and once you go back to your kingdom, you will have to apply these seven ideas learnt . . .'

Chanakya left the student thinking. The prince now understood why his father had sent him to the gurukul and why he was learning the *Arthashastra*—to become a great leader, the kind of a leader who understands not only good governance but also 'right thinking', aanvikshiki.

In this chapter we will look into the saptanga model in detail. We will call this the seven dimensions of thinking.

Once this model of thinking is learnt, it is easy to apply it immediately in our heads. The application becomes smooth. We get a sense of clarity about the role of the leader. By looking at these seven dimensions of thinking, one automatically starts thinking like a leader.

Let us understand each of the seven parts of a kingdom in detail. (A full chapter in the *Arthashastra* is dedicated to this topic—book six, chapter one, section ninety-six, titled 'Excellences of the Constituent Elements'.)

1. Swami (the king)
2. Amatya (the minister)
3. Janapada (the country)
4. Durga (the fortified city)
5. Kosha (the treasury)
6. Danda (the army)
7. Mitra (the ally)

Understanding these seven parts of a kingdom will give us seven dimensions in which to think about it.

1. Swami (the king)

The leader is the most important part of a kingdom. He or she can make or break an organization. Chanakya starts the saptanga model with the creation of a good leader. He knew how much everything depends on leadership and leadership thinking.

If you get this one person on top right, everything will fall into its place. He is the captain of the ship. The leader's main job is to give direction. Without a leader we do not know what to do.

2. Amatya (the minister)

The ministers form the second level of leadership, the king's core team. The ministers are the king's men and women.

They are also advisers to the king, and are also supposed to be good administrators. They have to be constantly alert, always in action and informed about what is happening everywhere in the kingdom. The ministers are the eyes and ears of the king.

3. Janapada (the country)

The citizens. If the king and the ministers are leading the kingdom, whom are they actually leading? The people. So without the citizens, there is no kingdom. Without followers, there is no leader. It is for the citizens that a kingdom exists. These are the people the leader has to take care of.

The attitude of a good leader is 'I exist to serve my people. In their happiness is my happiness. The people are my focus point. I would do anything for their well-being and prosperity.'

4. Durga (the fortified city)

The infrastructure. In the olden days, the citizens used to either live in villages or in cities (*rajadhani*). The capital cities were walled and entry into the capital was restricted. There were townships inside this fortified city, which constituted the main infrastructure of the kingdom.

The creation of good infrastructure was important for a leader. Inside the fortified city there used to be houses, water supplies and markets, where the citizens could engage in social and economic activities.

5. Kosha (the treasury)

A very important essential element of a kingdom. Managing the treasury properly is very much a key role of the leader. He has to make sure that revenue generation is adequate and expenditure is carefully measured. The role of the treasury in-charge (*kosha-adhyaksha*) is to keep the economy strong.

Good economic policies are decided by the swami along with his amatyas. Such economic polices help trade, the growth of industries, wealth creation and then wealth circulation and distribution.

6. Danda (the army)

A strong, well-managed army is the strength of a kingdom. The army not only protects the nation from external threats, but also from internal disturbances. A well-trained and well-equipped army also brings respect to the nation.

The army is not only military strength. The soldiers evoke a high level of patriotism among the masses as well. So, they are also role models for the citizens.

7. Mitra (the ally)

A kingdom is strong not only due to its internal growth, but also its foreign relations. A wise foreign policy is much needed, both in the good times and the bad. Allies help each other. Allies make you strong.

A leader is at the peak. But there are many peaks. So participating in building relations with other leaders is critical.

When we put the seven parts together, we can sum it up like so: 'A good leader, guided by good ministers, working for the happiness of the people, with good infrastructure, a full treasury, a strong and well-disciplined army and good foreign relations makes a great kingdom.'

This is big picture thinking. This is aanvikshiki.

Chanakya does not just tell us what. He also tells us how.

After explaining what the seven essential constituents of a kingdom are, he also shows us a path to create those seven constituents. He helps us to develop the essential seven dimensions of thinking.

The First Dimension of Thinking: Swami

A leader is required in every country, organization or team. But how do we identify a good leader? How do we create a good captain?

Chanakya now comes to the 'excellences of each of these seven constituents'. Excellences are the qualities that a person should have. If not, these can be identified and developed. Chanakya was a master of this art—the training of kings.

Therefore, he starts with creating an ideal leader (rajarishi).

He says:

> The excellences of the king are: born into a high family, endowed with good fortune, intelligence and spirit, given to seeing elders, pious, truthful in speech, does not break promises, grateful, liberal, of great energy, not dilatory, with weak neighbouring princes, resolute, not having a

mean council of ministers, desirous of training. These are the qualities of one easily approachable. (6.1.3)

These are some of the qualities that have been identified by Chanakya. With his sharp mind and strategic thinking, he would keep looking for such people with leadership potential.

Born into a high family: High here does not mean royal or of wealthy lineage. It means a family which has noble qualities. The value system of the family makes the person what he or she is. People born in such high families think many times before making a mistake. They have a legacy behind them. They need to stand up to the principles their forefathers held so dear.

Endowed with good fortune: It is quite interesting to note that Chanakya considers 'luck' or 'good fortune' important in leadership. The person who is at the right place at the right time indeed finds success very easily. The right person at the wrong place feels dejected. Also, good fortune is not only a matter of luck alone—it is the hard work of the past that suddenly bears fruit. Such fortunate people attract all good things easily towards them.

Intelligence and spirit: The leader has to be intelligent and also dynamic. Some only think and plan; others only keep doing without thinking. The best combination is 'plan out your work and work out your plan'. As the saying goes, if you fail to plan, you plan to fail. We need to have an ideal mix of planning and execution.

Given to seeing elders: Great leaders surround themselves with people greater than themselves. In the olden days (or even today), the true leaders keep getting guidance from their elders. These elders include the parents, the teachers and other noble people they come across. It is said that those who serve their elders will be always blessed with good fortune.

Pious, truthful in speech and does not break promises: A pious person is virtuous and well behaved. They have excellent moral character—essential in a leader. Also, a leader has to be trustworthy. Once they promise, they will deliver even at the cost of their lives. It is better to under-promise and over-deliver, rather than to over-promise and under-deliver. They speak the truth, but they also demonstrate truth in action.

Grateful, liberal, of great energy and not dilatory: Leaders are grateful and thankful to others for their success. Due to this, they are also humble by nature. They are also liberal in their thinking. With an open mind, they receive new ideas. They are free thinkers and appreciate original ideas. They believe in innovation and creativity and also have great energy. Leaders love to experiment. They are enthusiastic and make others around them also enthusiastic. They are not dilatory, slow or lazy. They take quick decisions and move ahead very fast.

With weak neighbouring princes, resolute, not having a mean council of ministers: The weakness of others can become our strength. So if a king has weak neighbours, he has many advantages. There are hardly any chances of the weaker king trying to attack a stronger one. The leader also has to be firm and resolute. The person at the top should be unwavering once the decision is taken. The leader should be selfless but also make sure his teams of ministers are also selfless; otherwise, they will give him the wrong advice.

Desirous of training, one easily approachable: Ever ready to learn is the quality of leadership. Leaders also give importance to training others. Leaders build the next generation of leaders. They are well trained and train others well too. They have an open-door policy. They are ever available to meet the person who requires his or her help and support. Leaders are large-hearted enough to accommodate everyone in their busy schedules.

The Second Dimension of Thinking: Amatya:

The selection of the leader is important. But equally important for Chanakya is the selection of the king's men—his team, his advisers and his close confidants. These are the amatyas, or the ministers.

Chanakya looks out for these qualities in identifying capable ministers:

A native of the country, of noble birth, easy to hold in check, trained in the arts, possessed of the eye (of science), intelligent, persevering, dexterous, eloquent, bold, possessed of a ready wit, endowed with energy and power, able to bear troubles, upright, friendly, firmly devoted, endowed with character, strength, health and spirit, devoid of stiffness and fickleness, amiable (and) not given to creating animosities—these are the excellences of a minister. (1.9.1)

A native of the country, of noble birth: The amatya has to be from the same place. Only then will he understand the problems at the grass-roots level. Besides, people native to the kingdom will always be more patriotic. This ensures commitment to nation-building. Again, noble birth (as with the swami) means that the value systems in the family are good. Character is first formed at our homes.

Easy to hold in check, trained in the arts, possessed of the eye (of science): Chanakya is warning us to be alert. The amatyas are entrusted with a lot of power, and there is always the danger that they will misuse that power. So keeping them in check becomes important. A minister also has to be very well trained, in various arts. This gives them a broader perspective. They should also be good thinkers with an eye for detail. And the science of politics should be part of their mental make-up.

Intelligent, persevering, dexterous, eloquent: Aanvikshiki—the training in right thinking—is also given to the amatyas. Intelligence is needed to guide the king. A good thinker can elevate the thinking of others. Also, ministers need to be persistent; they should not give up easily. They should also be dexterous—that is, agile and skilful. And furthermore, they should be good communicators. Their expressions and speech add to their personality.

Bold, possessed of a ready wit, endowed with energy and power: A minister has to have the courage to take necessary risks. He or she should also be witty by nature—clever and sharp. Such a person understands what has to be done in any situation. Additionally, he or she should be able to radiate energy and power. A confident person inspires confidence in others.

Able to bear troubles, upright, friendly, firmly devoted: Although he or she is confident and able to bear troubles, the minister should not be arrogant and unapproachable, but has to be friendly towards others. The minister has to be upright and trustworthy as far as dealings are concerned. Ministers should be firmly devoted to the king and the country that they represent.

Endowed with character, strength, health and spirit: There are different types of fitness: character fitness, physical strength and mental strength. Also, the minister should be healthy; healthy people think better. Instead of being busy tending to problems with their own bodies, ministers should be engaged in handling the problems of the country. Also, they should be of high spirits—ever ready to leap into action.

Devoid of stiffness and fickleness, amiable (and) not given to creating animosities: The minister should be flexible but not fickle. He or she should also be likeable and good-natured. He or she should also have the ability to attract others. The minister is in a position to affect the relationship between kings, even possibly kindle enmity, and so should not be given to creating animosities.

The Third Dimension of Thinking: Janapada

The country is the place where the people live. According to Chanakya, for a leader, the whole countryside (janapada) is to be included in his thinking. Not just the ones staying in cities—rather, the most attention should be given to the lower strata of society.

Chanakya goes one step further. He believes that the *praja* (citizens) of a kingdom include not just human beings, but also animals, birds, trees, water bodies and the mineral world. This is thinking with everyone and everything in mind. This is thinking in totality—aanvikshiki.

Keeping in mind the protection of the people living in rural areas, Chanakya lists the excellences of a country:

> Possessed of strong positions in the centre and at the frontiers, capable of sustaining itself and others in the times of distress, easy to protect, providing excellent means of livelihood, malevolent towards enemies, with weak neighbouring princes, devoid of mud, stones, salty grounds, uneven land, thorns, bands, wild animals, deer and forest tribes, charming,

endowed with agricultural land, mines, material forests and elephant forests, beneficial to cattle, beneficial to men, with protected pastures, rich in animals, not depending on rain for water, provided with water routes and land routes, with valuable, manifold commodities available in plenty, capable of bearing fines and taxes, with farmers devoted to work, with a wise master, inhabited mostly by lower varnas, with men loyal and honest—these are the excellences of a country. (6.1.8)

Possessed of strong positions in the centre and at the frontiers: The villages and the villagers require protection. In the countryside, especially in the border regions, enemies may seek to infiltrate the country. So, to keep the countryside possessed of a strong position is essential. Those villages which are centrally located and free from attacks prosper, and the people there are happier.

Capable of sustaining itself and others in the times of distress, easy to protect: There are many times when natural calamities happen. When such distress comes, the country should be able to protect itself. There are disaster management teams in the government departments now. But there should also be internal mechanisms to tackle disasters. When a disaster strikes, can the village protect itself? Thus, planning should ensure that it should be easy to protect.

Providing excellent means of livelihood: The primary reason for people to migrate is employment. If this is guaranteed, there will be a good ecosystem in a nation. Therefore, providing people with opportunities to earn by working hard is essential. Former President A.P.J. Abdul Kalam started a very good initiative named PURA (Providing Urban Amenities in Rural Areas), whereby the rural population would get all the benefits the city dwellers have.

Not depending on rain for water: For ages, India has been dependent on rainfall. The farmers work very hard and wait for the rains. If the rainfall is inadequate, their efforts are wasted. This is one of the many reasons for farmer suicides. So Chanakya says a janapada should not rely on the rains for water. Irrigation systems, water canals and rainwater harvesting all help.

With farmers devoted to work, with a wise master, with men loyal and honest: The quality of people residing in the country is more important than the quantity. Therefore, Chanakya suggests that those who are farmers are also devoted to their work. The culture and ethics of work is important in any organization or country. There should also be wise men in the villages. These are the personal guides and counsellors of the people; they ensure the men are loyal and honest.

The Fourth Dimension of Thinking: Durga

The layout of the fort and how to build it is the next priority. Chanakya gives a lot of thought to the creation of a durga.

A full section of the *Arthashastra* has been dedicated to this topic: book two, chapter three, section twenty-one, titled 'The Construction of Forts (Thirty-five Sutras)'.

The excellences of forts, Chanakya says, are:

> In all four quarters, on the frontiers of the country, he should cause a nature-made fortress, equipped for a fight, to be made: a water-front, (either) an island in the midst of water or high land shut in water; or a mountain fort, either consisting of rocks or a cave; or a desert fort, either one without water and shrubs or a salty region; or a jungle fort, either a marshy tract with water or a thicket of shrubs. (2.3.1)

Forts were created with multiple purposes.

Right from protecting the kingdom from external attacks to protecting the wealth of the nation in the treasury, this was also the place where the king, the ministers and the important people resided.

Let us elaborate of a few ideas that Chanakya said about creating an ideal durga.

He should cause a nature-made fortress, equipped for a fight: Chanakya made the forts in a way in which the maximum natural material was used. This also means his forts were made in the middle of nature. Nature thus became the biggest protector as well as the biggest source of raw material for the creation of a fortress and a fortified city. The fort should be well equipped to deal with an attack.

It should be amply stocked with weapons and other materials required in a battle.

He should cause channels to be made for storing goods (2.3.33): Storage facilities should be set up inside the durga, including for food and grains, for cattle feed, for the treasury, for jewels and other precious stones. The durga needs to be well provisioned during times of calamities, both natural (like earthquakes and floods) and man-made (like wars and other riots).

He should build in the centre of the city shrines and temples of gods (2.4.17): The Indian concept of town planning is deeply spiritual in nature. So temples were the centre of any village or city. The system exists even today, with cities named after temples: Kolkata (Kali Mata temple), Mumbai (Mumba Devi temple), Thiruvananthapuram (Anantha—temple of Vishnu), Madurai (temple of the goddess Madurai Meenakshi), Rameshwaram (temple of Rama).

This concept was integrated into architectural planning by Chanakya. The concept of temple cities took off in a major way and durgas were created based on these models.

The Fifth Dimension of Thinking: Kosha

This is probably the one dimension that we can call the essence of Chanakya's book.

He was one of the finest economic thinkers the world has produced. His financial strategies helped India to achieve the status of an economic superpower and made it the richest country in the world during those days.

Inside Chanakya's mind, there was an economist who was thinking continuously about the economic welfare of his nation. Additionally, he built the nation based not only on sound economic policies but also on spiritual principles.

So, what are the qualities of a good treasury?

> Acquired lawfully by the ancestors or by oneself, consisting mostly of gold and silver, containing various kinds of big jewels and cash, one that would withstand calamity even of a long duration in which there is no income—these are the excellences of a treasury. (6.1.10)

A treasury is the backbone of a nation or any organization. A strong, well-managed treasury is important for each and every person in the kingdom.

Let us look deep into what exactly he means.

Acquired lawfully by one's ancestors or by oneself: Chanakya was not just an economic thinker, but also a legal thinker. While he advocated the creation of wealth, he emphasized that it should be done within the bounds of the law. Now, sometimes, it may happen that one inherits a business which may not be very legal in nature. For instance, if your forefathers started a business that may not be paying taxes properly. So Chanakya suggests that even such activities started by ancestors should be cleaned up. This is the responsibility of the next generation.

Consisting mostly of gold and silver: The exchange of money today happens digitally, for the most part, having evolved over time from barter systems to coinage and currency notes. Chanakya was among the economists of his time who moved to replace the existing barter system with a formal structure in the form of coins. The mints he created had gold and silver coins for exchange and trading.

Containing various kinds of big jewels and cash: Our financial planning should include various diversified incomes. So after gold and silver, Chanakya suggested keeping a number of precious jewels. Similarly, one cannot just depend upon digital assets. A balance needs to be maintained, with physical assets forming an important part of one's portfolio. Additionally, some cash reserves are needed for emergencies.

One that would withstand calamity even of a long duration: Insurance is a concept that Chanakya was known to promote. He believed that bad times and calamities are bound to come. A clever person will be prepared to face it. So if trouble comes up, Chanakya would make his plans keeping in mind that it might last for a long time.

There is no income: There are days of sufficient income, there are days of poor income and there are days of no income. One should plan for these times. Savings have to be made. Imagine there is no income for a long time. What would you do? The treasury has to take care of the person (or the organization or the country). Today, we talk about retirement planning so that we can live comfortably even in our old age, when we have no fixed income to speak of.

The Sixth Dimension of Thinking: Danda

The army is vital to show others your strength. But the army should have both external and inner strength. The selection of soldiers and officers has to be done very carefully. Similarly, we have to recruit our employees carefully and then train them in the specific skills in order to keep productivity high.

Human beings are not just a resource, but the 'source' from where all activities start.

According to Chanakya, the qualities one should look for in an army are:

Inherited from the father and the grandfather, constant, obedient, with the soldiers' sons and wives contented, not disappointed during marches, unhindered everywhere, able to put up with troubles, has fought many battles, skilled in the science of all types of war and weapons, not having a separate interest because of prosperity and adversity shared with the king, consisting mostly of Kshatriyas—these are the excellences of an army. (6.1.11)

Inherited from the father and the grandfather: Once a soldier, always a soldier. Even if he retires, he will remain committed to the nation. Such people also inspire their family members to join the profession. There are various examples of many generations serving the army. So, Chanakya would give extra points to recruit people from the family of soldiers.

Constant, obedient: The mind of a soldier or an officer should not waver. It has to be constant. It has to be focused. The training given in the armed forces is actually a training of the mind. It is to discipline the person, make them obedient. The army saying goes, 'Ours is not to question how or why, ours is either to do or die.' Such an obedient army will achieve victory.

With the soldiers' sons and wives contented: Corruption starts at home. If a person brings in something beyond his or her income and the family refuses to accept it, then the person will not require more money. So, if the children and wife are content, they will live peacefully and will not demand anything beyond their means. Soldiers who are supported by their families will then be able to focus on the nation's glory.

Not disappointed during marches, able to put up with troubles: When the time comes to go to the battlefield, one cannot take a holiday. Also, while on a mission, the army will face many hardships. A strong force will not lose heart and abandon the march. The army and its leader have to find solutions to the problem and, with the available resources, achieve their goals.

Has fought many battles, skilled in the science of all types of war and weapons: An experienced solider is an asset. Those who have fought many battles know what happens in the field. A strong army consists of young, energetic soldiers at the lower rungs as well as a core of veteran campaigners. The combination brings great success. Additionally, they should be skilled in the use of different weapons in different types of wars. This can be achieved through training.

Not having a separate interest: 'The interest of the nation first, our team next, oneself last'—this is the motto the army lives by. Therefore, each person in the army should be selfless. There should be no disparate interests. If each of us puts the interests of the country first, we will have a great nation altogether.

The Seventh Dimension of Thinking: Mitra

Take help from others when offered, and help them in turn. Collaborate, focus on mutual development. Think of success for everyone. The final dimension of the saptanga way of thinking is mitra—the ally.

'Never fight the battle alone' is Chanakya's advice. Take a friend along with you. So, how do we select the right mitras?

Yet again, Chanakya's has a list of desirable qualities:

Allied from the days of father and grandfather, constant, under control, not having separate interest, great, able to mobilize quickly—these are the excellences of an ally. (6.1.12)

Allied from the days of father and grandfather: The concept of family friends comes up here. If you have people who have been friends with your family for several generations, the relationship is one that has stood the test of time. Imagine a friend who been with you since childhood and now, after you have grown old, the friendship continues. The bond you share will be strong. Among nations too there are long-lasting friendships. The previous generations were friends and the leaders of this generation also maintain those friendships.

Constant, under control: The test of real friendship is during the bad times. In prosperity, everyone becomes your friend, but in adversity you know who your real friends are. Therefore, a constant friend is to be trusted, says Chanakya. Also, a friend is one who has self-control—they will save you from bad habits where others may introduce you to vices.

Able to mobilize quickly: A good ally should become a great ally. Someone we can look to as a role model, someone who walks the talk. When you need it, they should be able to mobilize resources quickly. In the friendship among nations, we find that if there is some natural disaster like an earthquake, the allies immediately send aid. And during war, they send their forces to support us.

The seven dimensions of thinking are a unique, holistic model. However, Chanakya was always self-critical. After perfecting the saptanga model, he put his mind to analysing its flaws. Was there anything he had missed while visualizing the perfect nation?

He applied aanvikshiki himself and found a new dimension. We shall find out about this eighth dimension of thinking in the next chapter.

5

The Eighth Dimension of Thinking

We just studied the saptanga, the seven dimensions of thinking.

However, Chanakya was a detailed thinker. He would ask himself, 'Why are these seven elements required? What is their purpose?'

And this was the answer he provided himself: to defeat the enemy. It is for defeating and protecting oneself from the enemy that we need to make the seven dimensions of thinking clear and strong.

To plan everything from the point of view of one's enemy is the eighth dimension of thinking.

In this chapter we will see what, according to Chanakya, went into thinking about the enemy and the competition, and what he did to ensure he was not defeated under any circumstances.

If we truly understand Chanakya, we will never have to deal with failure. Success is guaranteed. This is because he does not take the enemy for granted. He knows that the enemy will be thinking about us and ahead of us. It is crucial to get into the mind of the enemy, and to understand the enemy even before he or she understands us.

Therefore, it is important to study the enemy. There are many techniques, theories, principles, strategies, tactics and formulas that he used to defeat a very strong enemy. We will learn some of them in this chapter.

War is a mind game, and Chanakya knew this very well.

As the saying goes, 'The more you sweat in peace, the less you bleed in war.'

To begin with, let us see what Chanakya considers to find the weakness of the enemy.

The Eighth Dimension of Thinking—The Enemy

Many things come in sets of seven: the seven wonders of the world, the seven notes in music, the seven seas, the seven colours of the rainbow, among others. Our search is always for the eighth wonder. In trying to find the eighth dimension, we leap into the unknown.

Chanakya looks at the enemy and finds weaknesses. He says:

> Not of royal descent, greedy, with a mean council of ministers, with disaffected subjects, unjust in behaviour, not applying himself (to duties), vicious, devoid of energy, trusting in fate, doing whatever pleases him, without shelter, without a following, impotent, ever doing harm to others—these are the excellences of the enemy. For an enemy of this type becomes easy to exterminate. (6.1.12)

The system of SWOT analysis is quite popular in the management field. It stands for:

- S: Strength
- W: Weakness
- O: Opportunities
- T: Threats

With the SWOT formula, we will be able to diagnose the enemy better. We need to understand his or her strengths as well as weaknesses. As Chanakya would say, 'In the strength of the enemy lies his weakness.'

Once we find the weakness of the enemy, we have a competitive advantage. We use this advantage to conquer the enemy. We will now study Chanakya's statement in detail.

Not of royal descent: People born in royal families have a natural advantage. They get training in leadership right from their birth. Since they are born with a silver spoon, they do not have to worry about basic survival. Additionally, the environment in which they grow up helps them learn strategy, during the formal and informal discussions they have at home.

If an enemy does not have this natural advantage, he or she has to learn everything right from the beginning. Chanakya would say that such an enemy has a disadvantage—which can be our advantage.

Greed: A greedy enemy is easy to defeat. There are many types of greed—for money, for power and sometimes for name and fame. As Mahatma Gandhi said, there is enough in this world for everyone's need, but not for everyone's greed. Greed is very dangerous. Once we set off to get more than what we need, it is an endless journey.

In a power game, if Chanakya understood that the person was possessed with greed, it played to his advantage. One can bribe the person in one form or another. This is easy. To offer more power and benefits is like getting the enemy into a quicksand: once caught, it will only pull him or her down; there is no escape.

With a mean council of ministers: If the enemy is not greedy, take a look at his team. His team consists of his council of ministers and advisers. If the strategy does not work with the top man, try your methods with the second level of leaders. If these ministers are mean and selfish— bingo! Your strategy is now working. Now you know where to attack.

If plan A to bribe the number one is not working, don't lose heart. The plan B with his mean council of ministers will help. Also, ministers are sometimes more powerful than the king. They also advise the king. Once they are on your side, they will give wrong advice to their leader, and you have a strategic advantage over the enemy.

With disaffected subjects: If the subjects of the enemy are disaffected, meaning unconcerned and uninvolved in any affairs of the state, it shows the enemy is weak. This also indicates the lack of good governance. The people lead their own self-centred lives, indulging in their own selfish activities. There is hardly any national feeling or patriotism.

They may not pay taxes; there is bound to be corruption in the system. Things will be easy if there is an enemy kingdom like that. The way to conquer such an enemy is by convincing the people to take your side. Chanakya would create a split in the minds of the subjects. Then he would encourage a mass movement against the state power, and a public revolt would lead to the defeat of the enemy.

Unjust behaviour: Being just is the quality of a good leader. People love just leaders. Such a leader is honoured and appreciated by his or her followers. An unjust leader is hated by his or her subjects. When it comes to justice, if one does not get a fair trial and decisions are autocratic in nature, the leader is considered tyrannical.

The leader is automatically considered undemocratic. Democracy is not just a form of governance, but also the attitude of the leader. In the olden days, when monarchy was the form of government, most kings would still consider public opinion and resolve matters in a mutually respectful manner. If the enemy does not have these qualities, he is very vulnerable, easy to attack and win over.

Application (to duties): We Indians have always believed in duties over rights. The understanding that each person should do his or her duty is very much part of our thinking. Parents do their duties for their children, the teacher for his or her students, and citizens for their country. The duty of one person is the right of the other person. If duties are fulfilled, rights are automatically met.

Inside Chanakya's mind, one would find a duty-centric approach to leadership. A leader who does not do his duties is not accepted by him. The king should always be aware of his duties. By not applying himself to the duties of a king (raja dharma), the king sends a wrong message to the world. If the enemy king forgets his duties, or is unmindful of them, then he is a weak king, easy to win over.

Vicious: With great power comes great responsibility. But a powerful person can also be irresponsible. If this awareness of responsibilities is absent, there is misuse of power. Such a person tends to become vicious. He can be brutal and inhuman in dealing with others. The punishments would be unjust. And sometimes a sadistic mindset gets created. They can even go on a rampage of killing people.

There are many instances in history, as well in modern times, where leaders have executed and killed others just to show their power, to keep up their ideologies or belief systems. Chanakya dealt with these kinds of leaders in a powerful yet diplomatic manner. To dethrone such a leader was his specialty. The way he dethroned Dhanananda, the last king of the Nanda dynasty, is worth a study.

Devoid of energy: A lazy enemy is loved by Chanakya. Such a person does not take any action, initiate any new projects and does not like to maintain things that have been acquired. Anything related to progress is not considered worth taking up. He or she loves the status quo. Such leaders stagnate. And stagnation is a sure recipe for disaster.

Such enemies are devoid of energy and can depress the people around them. Imagine a group of sheep led by a lion—the group of sheep will become active. Think the opposite, a group of lions led by a sheep. The lions will lose all their drive and energy. An unenthusiastic leader can easily be defeated by the enemy. Such kingdoms where the leader is lazy can be captured without much effort and in less time.

Trusting in fate: Another form of laziness is trusting in fate. There is a big difference between destiny and the hard work you need to get there. Even to meet one's destiny, one needs to put in effort. A person trusting in fate does nothing. Waiting for good luck to take care of one's life is the worst planning one can do. 'What you meet in life is destiny, how you meet it is self-effort,' said Swami Chinmayananda, the great spiritual leader. Fate plays a role in our lives, but trusting only in fate is dangerous. Chanakya would love to have an enemy who waits for the god of luck to bless him. He knows that inside the mind of such a person lies a totally effortless person, easy to conquer.

Doing whatever pleases him: Leaders are supposed to think of all possible consequences before taking action. They must think several times before doing anything. Doing anything without thinking can be harmful. Such impulsive leaders destroy whatever has been created. If you ask a leader why he or she is doing something, one really does not expect the answer to be 'Because I like it.'

What is beneficial for the people, what will be good for the work undertaken, what is moral and ethical, what will give progress—that is the kind of work that has to be done. The leader should act for his personal benefit. So, if there is an enemy who is impulsive, it is an advantage, Chanakya says. He can be easily defeated as well.

Without shelter: Shelter is very essential. A place to stay, a house for oneself, a property of our own—these give a person a sense of stability. Gypsies keep moving around; vagabonds and nomads have no stability. They have nothing to call their own. Such people can be easily driven out of a place.

An enemy who does not have a shelter does not have a big enough reason to fight. There is no place he can call his own. So, what is he fighting for? There is no country to protect; there is no feeling of patriotism. There is no higher purpose to die for. Therefore, such enemies give up easily in fights. They do not continue fighting, as there is hardly any reason to fight.

Without a following: Only if one has followers can one call oneself a leader. What is a leader without followers? Then it is just self-claimed leadership. The person may want to get into a leadership position, but if there are no followers, there is no one who will fight for that person. Leadership is determined by the number of people who can stand up for your cause. People should be ready to walk on water for the sake of their leader.

What is a teacher without good students? This applies to leadership too. Leadership and followers go hand in hand. They are two sides of the same coin. They exist mutually. As leaders require followers, so do followers require leaders. Such leadership with a strong following is not easy to defeat. The reverse is what Chanakya likes in an enemy.

Impotent: Some people are taken for granted. They are the kind of leaders who are considered useless, ineffective and unproductive. People do not fear such leaders. Such leaders are useless. Even though the leader has a strong army, he will never give orders to attack. There is a lot of frustration among the subjects when a leader is like that. Such leaders do not attract good people to work with them. Instead, the good people start leaving them.

For Chanakya, such an enemy king is a dream. He does not have to spend his time, effort, money or send a large army to defeat such a king. The impotent leader is already lost. He understands failures more than success. There is nothing required to be done to a person who is impotent. Such a leader cannot even handle success.

Ever doing harm to others: Some leaders enjoy harming others. They never think of doing good, but only of doing something bad and disastrous. They are the criminals in society. They add no value wherever they go, or whatever they do. They only bring nuisance, irritation and frustration to others' lives.

Some people spread happiness wherever they go; leaders like these, however, make others happy whenever they go. So defeating such a king and eliminating him is a dream to his own people. Therefore, such enemy kings are easy to fight and easy to defeat.

If the above qualities are present in an enemy, it is considered excellent for Chanakya. Even if one of these qualities is present, it is easy to defeat the enemy. 'Build on the weakness of the enemy' is the mantra of Chanakya. The more weaknesses in the enemy, the better.

Inside his mind, Chanakya created an excellent espionage system to collect information and find the weaknesses of the enemy. The concept of *vishkanya*, today known as the honeytrap, is quite relevant in this context. The informers and spies would gather enough facts about the enemy for Chanakya to decide his course of action to eliminate the enemy. Success comes not only through our strengths but the weakness of others—Chanakya understood that. So should all of us. For an enemy of this type becomes easy to exterminate.

For Chanakya, everything is easy. He was very studious as a student and excellent as a teacher. As a strategist, he did his research well. He would gather all the facts and evidences, verify them with information from different sources, re-check and re-examine if required, and only then would he come up with a plan.

Once the plan was ready, he would execute it flawlessly. Thus having listed down the enemy's various weaknesses, he was pretty sure that it was easy to exterminate him. Unfortunately, most people do not like to plan and study in detail. They want success without effort. This is where Chanakya stands apart.

Chanakya would take his time, spend time thinking and then come up with out-of-the-box solutions to a problem.

Competition Is Good

When we think about competition, there is a negative feeling. We do not like competition. But Chanakya was different; he liked competition. He believed that having an enemy keeps you alert. There are many good things about having an enemy, having a competitor. Competition is good, because it brings out the best in you.

Do not just look at the enemy as a person; it can be a problem, a situation or a challenge that you have come across. You have to face it, tackle it and come up with a solution to the problem.

One day, one of Chanakya's friends from a different kingdom came to him. He looked very sad and had some issues in that kingdom. He looked at Chanakya and said, 'Sir, my kingdom has a major problem with the government employees and the bureaucrats. The state administration is totally corrupt. Because of this, there is no progress in our place and people are frustrated. Please do something, tell us what to do.'

Chanakya was not an impulsive person. He took his time to think through the situation, look at the problem in depth, look at the ground realities and only then did he make an action plan. This is how Chanakya operated. Inside his mind was a solution-focused approach, but one that relied on studying details.

He said, 'Okay. Let us go to your kingdom. I want to see the situation myself, and then see how to solve it.'

This friend of Chanakya's then took him to his kingdom. He took Chanakya to various government offices, marketplaces and also the common people's houses. He could see the degree of corruption that was evident even in public places. The situation was very alarming indeed. Anybody could tell that the administration was in a really bad shape.

Chanakya was thoughtful for a long time. He suddenly asked his friend, 'Tell me, what percentage of people in the government offices are corrupt?'

This came as a surprise to his friend. 'Percentage?'

He wondered. His first impulse was to tell Chanakya that '100 per cent of the people are corrupt'. But he paused and started thinking. There were people in the system who were still not bitten by the heavy corruption all around. These honest officials worked sincerely for the people even though others in the government machinery did not like them. They were a rare few, but they did exist.

And he told Chanakya, 'About 98 per cent of people in this system are corrupt.'

Chanakya gave an alarmingly wide smile. He seemed to be laughing, when his friend interrupted, saying, 'Sir, I know why you are laughing. The situation is hopeless, right? If 98 per cent of the people in the system are like this, then you can't do anything. Is that right?'

Chanakya, in a happy mood, said, 'No, no, no. I am not worried about the 98 per cent who are corrupted. I am happy that 2 per cent of the people working in the government offices are still untouched by corruption. They are our hope. These are the people we should be focusing on. In total darkness, there is some light at the end of the tunnel.'

His friend was taken aback by how Chanakya saw situations so differently.

And then came Chanakya's final suggestion to his friend, 'My challenge is to see how I can increase the percentage of people who are honest and sincere. Can we make the number of honest people 98 per cent in the system?'

And he made an action plan in his mind. 'Can you arrange a meeting with the 2 per cent? They will show you the way forward.'

Chanakya always tackled his enemies and competition with such a positive mindset.

Shatru—The Enemy

There are many positive sides of the *shatru*, according to Chanakya. If you develop this kind of mindset, there will be a paradigm shift in your thinking.

1. He brings out the best in you

Till there is a problem or a challenge, we take things for granted. When an enemy comes to attack us, we cannot be lazy; we need to fight the enemy. You are pushed to act. Thus, the shatru will bring out the best in you.

With the limited resources in hand, in the limited time we have, we need to work out a solution. There is no room for procrastination. We need to act quickly and come up with methods and strategies to eliminate the enemy.

2. The sleeping giant will awaken

In the Ramayana, there is the story of a warrior named Kumbhakarna. He used to sleep for six months, and eat for the remaining six. There was no purpose in his life, even though he was among the best warriors in the kingdom of Lanka. When Rama attacked Lanka, Ravan, Kumbhakarna's brother, gave orders to wake him up to fight the enemy. Once the sleeping giant was up, it was a tough fight for the attackers.

Similarly, we may be enjoying life—eating, drinking, making merry and sleeping. But once the enemy attacks, the sleeping giant inside us has to be awakened. We can no longer take things for granted. Then we do our best and fight the competitor.

3. Challenges make you strong

It is good to have challenges. Taking up a challenge with a positive spirit can make you stronger. Yes, it may be an unknown path that you are taking for the first time. But, with a positive spirit, you will able to emerge successful. A challenge is a double-edged sword. It can make you weak or it can make you strong.

Take a deep breath. Face the challenge and make things happen. Your inner strength and confidence can do wonders. There are people who come from humble backgrounds. Yet, they take up the challenges they are faced with, and from ordinary, they go on to become extraordinary. These role models inspire many others to emerge stronger with challenges.

4. A push is required

We may know a lot of motivational theories about taking up challenges. Yet sometimes an external or internal push is required. It is best to have an internal push—the self-motivated people do this. However, most of us require an external push. The mentor, the coach, the guide and the friend will all serve this purpose.

When we learn swimming, the role of the coach is very critical for this external push. He will help you learn the basic steps and make you practise in water. But, one day, he will suddenly push you into the water—there you learn swimming in the real sense. The coach is watching, but you have to do it yourself.

Study of Espionage Systems

The spying systems created by Chanakya are quite amazing. The intelligence he gathered through the spies were very much required for him to make his attack plan against the enemies. Based on this information, strategies were developed by Chanakya to win in any given condition.

In the *Arthashastra*, there is a detailed study of the espionage systems Chanakya created—book one, chapter twelve, section seven, called 'Appointment of Roving Spies', and section eight, titled 'Rules for Secret Servants'. There are quite a few insights we can gather about the robust systems Chanakya created.

But, before looking at some technical aspects of the spying system, let us look at a story about Chanakya gathering information from the vishkanya while he planned his attack against Alexander, who was on his way to conquer the world.

Alexander came from Greece. He was on a mission and had almost conquered half of the world. His next step was India. India, at that time, was divided into sixteen regional kingdoms, all at war.

Chanakya saw that Alexander would become the biggest threat to India, and went around uniting various kings and their kingdoms to fight against him. Some supported him, while others did not. Chanakya was neither a king nor did he have his own army. Yet, by strategically using all the information he had gathered, he defeated his foreign enemy.

He did not have his own army, but by bringing together the army of others, he put together a large force, seeing which the soldiers of Alexander's army were shocked and frightened. Even if we do not have resources of our own, we can gain victory by using the resources of others. Collaboration was the method Chanakya used to achieve victory.

Chanakya had heard that Alexander's army was made of superior warriors, who had different weapons and were completely committed to the vision of their leader. It would not be easy to defeat them. They were said to be divine and to have heavenly blessings.

Chanakya knew that if a common man heard such descriptions, he was sure to be gripped by fear. Even before the war had started, the soldiers would mentally accept defeat. Chanakya wanted correct information, not exaggerated accounts.

For this he sent a female spy into the enemy camp. These spies, named vishkanyas, were trained in understanding human psychology. When they came back to Chanakya, he wanted to know all the details in order to make his plan. An intelligent person is one who sees what is not shown, listens to what is not being said and reads between the lines.

Chanakya understood that Alexander's men, though very strong and determined, were far away from their families, and they longed to be back home. He knew that the weak point of any soldier was the family that he misses.

Chanakya then first attacked the psyche of the Greek soldiers and demotivated them. Among the Greeks, along with the fear of the huge army that they saw, there was now also the desire to go back home—which was the turning point in the battle.

The Female Spies

Chanakya was very careful in selecting the right people for the right job. Like a farmer who selects the right seeds before sowing, he wanted the best people to gather information for him.

There were multiple types of spies employed by Chanakya. We will look into one of the selection processes for the female spies.

Women think differently from men. They have a different way of looking at a particular person or situation.

The female spies were selected by Chanakya based on the following:

A wandering nun, seeking a secure livelihood, poor, widowed, both Brahmin by caste and treated with honour in the palace, should frequently go to the houses of high officers. By her office are explained similar offices for the shaven nuns of heretical sects. (1.12.4)

Chanakya would understand the needs of a woman, and the different categories that they belonged to. Based on those aspects, he would look out for his informers.

A wandering nun: Female monks were prevalent during Chanakya's times. They used to go from one place to another and were given entry into every village. In Indian culture, monks, ascetics and sanyasis are always respected and welcomed. They are seen as messengers of peace and spiritual advice.

However, for Chanakya, they were also a rich source of information. These monks were in touch with the ground reality, and thus became the king's eyes and ears. It is not possible to gather all information through government agencies alone. Groups like the order of monks will give access to easy information as they have access to all types of people—from the classes to the masses.

Seeking a secure livelihood: Even monks and ascetics require basic requirements for survival—food, clothing and shelter. Chanakya knew that even the wandering nuns would, of course, require a secure livelihood. Such nuns were the people he wanted to recruit into his espionage network. They would get the secure income they needed and he would get the required intelligence.

Poor, widowed: Of the women in this tradition of nuns, some would be very poor and some widowed. They would require some social support. Not just financially but also morally. A safe and secure environment is needed by these women. Chanakya would look into making them socially secure.

Now, look at a new dimension. A widow would also get a new purpose in life. Not just social support but social dignity when she gets into employment. A widow may require financial assistance for herself and her family. So such a person in need is also helped.

Both Brahmin by caste and treated with honour in the palace: Brahmins are the intellectual class of the society. In the ancient Indian system of caste, Brahmins were considered so not by birth, but by their qualities and abilities. Brahmin women, highly intelligent and educated, were recruited for gathering information. They would have original thoughts, and provide better insights than the rest.

Chanakya would take care of the honour of these women. They would also be treated with honour in the court. The female spies would enter the chamber of the kings with dignity and could not be misused. They could even sit down with the high officials and debate with them to gather necessary information.

Should frequently go to the houses of higher officials: Not just the palaces, these women were required to go to the houses of higher officials of the state. Networking did not happen just at the palaces, but also at homes. While at home we get to know the person in a totally different setting— sometimes, the person at the workplace and the person at home are two contrasting personalities.

Even by simply looking at the house, these female spies could gather a lot of information. The financial situation is also better understood at home. While interacting with the other members of the family, we come to understand the family culture. Being women, these spies could even discuss matters with the other ladies of the family. Also, being nuns, they tried to get spiritual solutions to their problems. Thus, a whole new world of information opened up in front of them.

By her office are explained similar offices for the shaven nuns of heretical sects: Now, this type of wandering nuns being involved in espionage is just the tip of the iceberg.

Chanakya used many such systems. There was a government department dedicated to these wandering nun spies. Chanakya mentions that similar government offices for the shaven nuns of heretical and other sects also existed.

Their operations were different from those of the wandering nuns.

How to Attack the Enemy

We will now see how Chanakya used the information gathered through the spies to plan his attacks.

Out of the fifteen books in Kautilya's *Arthashastra*, seven are dedicated to war and its methods.

During Chanakya's time, wars were a constant reality. The king had to always be prepared for either internal wars or external threats.

Chanakya did not want his students to sit idle. Even during peacetime, he was getting ready for war. He was ever prepared for the worst situation.

Chanakya had different methods of teaching war techniques. One of them was by playing war games, both physical and mental. At the physical level, he wanted the king and his army to be fit. So he sent them on training and also hunting games. The hunting games proved useful since animals were commonly used in war.

At the mental level, he prepared them to continuously think of warfare strategies. Therefore, he invented the game of chess.

Chess

The game of chess is very interesting. It is like a simulation exercise, played before the actual moves happen.

In the game of chess, we have two players with equal strength. The elephants, the camels, the soldiers and the horses are all in equal number. Thus, the winner is not determined by the numbers you have on your side, but by the calculated moves that you make against the opponent.

This game was called 'chaturanga' (four components of an army), which later became 'shatrang' and is now called chess.

Even today, chess includes the four basic components that Chanakya had conceived of.

C – chariots
H – horses
E – elephants
SS – soldiers

The mind game called chess can be very useful in the real game of war. Battles are, after all, said to be fought not in the battlefield, but in the minds of the generals.

This strategic preparation guaranteed success against the enemy. This is also aanvikshiki.

The Four Basic Strategies

Chanakya is known for his profound strategies. But he is also known for his simplification of these war strategies to ensure victory.

The famous four basic strategies of Chanakya are: sama, dana, danda and bheda.

He uses these four principles during different situations in war:

That which the other might seize by force, he should offer through one of the means (sama, dana, danda, bheda). He should preserve his body, not wealth; for, what regret can there be for wealth that is impermanent? (12.1.32)

If an enemy has taken away something by force, it does not mean you have to use force against him too. Force is not the only option. Try any of the four options given below:

1. Sama (discussion)

It is not necessary to attack an enemy straightaway. Just try to discuss the matter. If issues can be resolved by diplomatic talks, why go to war at all? For every war that takes place, there are one thousand that have been avoided by discussion and understanding.

2. Dana (material benefit for the opponent)

There could be material benefit that the opponent wants. It is better to offer that benefit if it will avoid war. A lot of wealth and several lives are lost in every war. However, trade, business exchanges and economic policies also can make us win over the enemy.

3. Danda (punishment or attack)

If diplomacy does not work, it is time to attack. It could be a silent war, which is never understood by the opponent. Or, it could be a direct attack to show the enemy our power. There are various types of attacks, including guerrilla warfare and biological attacks. Today cyber wars are also quite common between nations.

4. Bheda (division within the enemy camp)

Divide and rule—this policy is preferred by Chanakya. Split the enemy into various parts. Let them bleed through a thousand cuts. Taking a person from the enemy camp into your side can be more fruitful in this divide and rule policy.

Which of these four principles is to be used and when depends on the demand of the situation? No two situations are the same. So, wisdom needs to be applied in order to reach the right strategy. This is situational leadership.

The Final Suggestion

A time comes in war when you have to choose. Sometimes the choice is between the cost of your life and the wealth you could give away.

It is most important to save one's own life even at the cost of giving up all of one's wealth.

> He should preserve his body, not wealth; for, what regret can there be for wealth that is impermanent. (12.1.32)

No matter what happens, do not give up the body. Avoid death. If there is life, everything will come back. Even lost wealth can be regained. For wealth is impermanent and there will be no regret saving one's own life, even at the cost of giving up wealth.

Now, this does not mean the person is a runaway warrior. This is a very strategic call—it is short-term loss for the sake of long-term gain.

We save our lives and break free from the clutches of the enemy. Even if we are defeated, we do not accept it; we start planning another attack. Even in exile, the king should not waste time and effort. He should prepare for the next chance to attack his enemy. Preparing for the next big action too is aanvikshiki.

6

The Other Side of Chanakya

Shrewd, cunning, wicked, thick-skinned, stony-hearted, cold-blooded—these are some of the words that are still used for Chanakya.

Chanakya wrote his *Arthashastra* under the name Kautilya (a person with *kuta niti*, meaning immoral strategies). This negative side of Chanakya is quite well known.

So what was really going on inside Chanakya's mind while crafting the many policies that are considered not entirely ethical?

To explain this, let me share a story connected to Chanakya's life that gives us an indication of his attitude while promoting such policies.

A dear friend of Chanakya who was visiting the Magadha kingdom was staying with him.

During an informal conversation, the friend asked Chanakya, 'Why is that people hate you, are afraid of you, and consider you a man who cannot be trusted?'

This concerned friend knew the real Chanakya since they were childhood friends, when he was known as Vishnugupta—his original name.

'Vishnu, I know you are not like that. You are a person who is most loving by nature, very concerned about the welfare of all; there is nothing but care and love for others. Then why is it that people have misunderstood you?'

Chanakya started laughing. 'Listen, I am not in the popularity game. And it does not matter to me what they say to my face or behind my back. People have their own views. For me, the purpose of my life is greater than what the perception about me is.'

These were profound insights that Chanakya gave his dear friend.

'The purpose of your life?' The friend was stunned, and wanted to know what was inside Chanakya's mind.

'Yes, I am clear on the purpose for which I was born. Nothing can distract me from achieving my goal. I am focused and determined to achieve that before I leave this planet. So, to attain that, whatever is required, I will do it. No means is right or wrong for me. Finally, I will accomplish it.'

Seeing the fire in Chanakya's eyes, the friends asked, 'Can I know what the goal is?'

With a deep breath Chanakya said, 'Nation-building.' He continued to explain. 'We are all born in a great place—Bharat. Our ancestors were great men and women of wisdom and realization. Ours is a spiritual culture. It helps man to achieve the ultimate—the realization of God. Our rishis, munis, sadhus and sanyasis gave the world invaluable gifts like meditation, yoga and Ayurveda. We have made all knowledge available to the world without any personal interests. This is the place where even gods feel lucky to have taken birth. But . . .' There was a pause filled with a feeling of sadness.

He continued, 'There are a few people in our country who are criminals. Unfortunately, these few people in our generation also happen to be kings and leaders. Once society is led by criminals and selfish people, there is no happiness among the subjects. There is only frustration and hopelessness . . .'

And then reminding his friend, Chanakya said, 'I was born to a great teacher of rajaniti, Rishi Chanak—my father. You knew him very well. He was a great man and advised the kings on good governance and leadership. Unfortunately, he had to pay a price—his life itself . . . I decided to take up what my father had left incomplete. So when I advised the kings based on our scriptures, I realized that they did not care for anything. There was only selfishness in their approach. Corruption was everywhere and there was no way to guide them.'

Then he revealed his strategy: 'So I decided to create a new king. A new leader, Chandragupta, who would follow the way of dharma. And all those who came in the way, I eliminated them using kuta niti. Sometimes for the sake of the protection of the good, the evil has to be eliminated.'

His friend was aware that there was a softer side to Chanakya that hardly anyone knew of. He only had respect for Chanakya.

Chanakya's concern for the welfare of all beings is reflected throughout the *Arthashastra*. We will cover five aspects that shows us the softer side of Chanakya:

1. Relations matter
2. Taking care of old people
3. Women's empowerment

4. Respect for teachers
5. Letting go of the enemy

One must note that his concern was for all beings, not just humans. It included plants, the animal kingdom as well as the water bodies and the mineral world. The heart of a person who has achieved realization is large enough to accommodate the whole world.

1. Relations Matter

Human beings have a sense of belonging to a family and to society.

We human beings live in an interdependent society. We require each other. Without the support of each other, we cannot achieve anything. The walk may be lonely, but if you have a companion, you will enjoy the journey much more.

Great people like Chanakya knew this. They knew that even at the individual level or at the national level, relations matter the most. Therefore, in the *Arthashastra* 'foreign relations' is given importance.

Please note there is a big difference between 'foreign policy' and 'foreign relations'. Even though the two are interconnected, they are different. A person can have a good foreign policy, but without good foreign relations, there is no way he can implement that policy.

India getting the United Nations to declare 21 June as the International Yoga Day was a master stroke in foreign policy. It was possible only due to the foreign relations India has built over the years.

Thus, foreign relations become a game-changing strategy towards success. Therefore, building relations was critical for Chanakya.

He adds that relations with insiders are just as important as relations with outsiders. Chanakya is thinking continuously about the kind of people he will have to deal with, while facing different types of enemies. Having a set of good friends and supporters on your side is definitely an advantage.

So Chanakya suggests:

> He should establish contacts with forest chieftains, frontier-chiefs and chief officials in the cities and the countryside. (1.16.7)

Leaders associate with other leaders. A king may be number one in his kingdom. But he should be aware that there are many others who are mini-kings in his kingdom. Only if they support the main king will he remain in power.

What kind of leadership relations should the king then maintain?

He should establish contacts: Relations have to be built; they do not just happen. A lot of effort goes into building and maintaining a relationship. Just because two people are together does not mean they have a good relationship. And just because two people are separated by distance does not mean they do not have good relations. The distance between hearts is more important than physical distance. And in today's world, technology can help us build relations.

Chanakya suggests that the leader should be proactive. He or she must take active steps to build a relationship. Contacts have to be maintained on a regular basis. One of the key duties of the administration is to maintain good public relations.

With forest chieftains: The forest is usually far away from the capital city, which is where the king stays. The king will never have a direct control over the forest. The forests are controlled by the forest chiefs. The tribal leaders and community leaders—all of them control and lead their own groups. These forest chiefs are the decision-makers in their respective regions. They are the ones who would understand the land and its various productions. Be it the forest produce, the minerals, the water bodies or the flora and fauna—everything is understood by them.

The people dwelling in the forests will listen to the forest chiefs only, not the king sitting in the capital. Chanakya understood this; therefore, he tried to have friendly relations with the forest chiefs. When the king has to accomplish anything in the forest, these leaders will aid him. Listen to the forest chiefs and they will show you the path to success.

Frontier-chiefs: The frontiers of a kingdom are important places. These frontiers are the border states or villages. They define the boundaries of the kingdom. They might share borders with a neighbouring kingdom too. And that neighbour could be an enemy.

Many activities happen in these border areas—trade, exchange of goods and even import and exports. Some of them might even be illegal. The smuggling of goods happens at the frontier, not to mention infiltration by refugees.

Chanakya knew that maintaining good relations with frontier chiefs is essential for keeping border security in place. These frontier chiefs are very vulnerable also. The enemy kings might try to offer them bribes and even positions of power. So winning them over means protecting the entire kingdom.

Some frontiers include the sea, mountains, deserts and even forests. Even today, people in these regions are recruited by the armed forces for protection of the nation. Organizations like the Border Security Force (BSF) are examples of this.

Chief officials in the cities: The government is run by the state machinery. And the machinery is run by the officers of the government. In modern India, these are the civil service officers—the Indian Administrative Services (IAS) and the Indian Police Service (IPS) officers.

Chanakya suggests that one should maintain relations with these officers. Usually, these senior officers control their junior officers and administrative staff. The senior officers sit in the cities or the state capital.

These people are very well informed. They know about the system and the complete workings of the kingdom. Instead of just considering them as servants of the king, the king should maintain relations with them. In formal and informal discussions with them, the king will learn about the happenings in the kingdom. The government officials are the ears and eyes of the king. And also its hands and legs.

Chief officials of the countryside: Like the officers in the city, the government officials in the villages or the countryside are another group of important people. They are the ones who run the government machinery in the rural areas. Mahatma Gandhi once said, 'India lives in villages.'

The statement is true even in the modern days. The villages with their panchayati raj system are the backbone of India. We have nearly six lakh villages in this country. The majority of the population still lives in rural areas, so good governance has to go down to the villages as well.

Till the last man in the last village is happy, the work of the government is not done. So how does Chanakya ensure success in the rural regions? Through the chief officials in the countryside. These officials understand the village culture, tradition as well as their native languages.

The British had used this policy while ruling over India. They made the native people the officers in the administrative system and through them they ruled all over India.

2. Taking Care of Old People

Old people—are they assets or liabilities?

If we look purely from an economic standpoint, they may prove to be a financial burden, especially if there are no savings or retirement plans in place.

But Chanakya and his economic models are different. He would put the old people on the asset side of the nation. Even though they may not be bringing in income, they have invaluable wisdom. Their knowledge and experience can create wonders.

There are many instances where retired people have proven more valuable than young, energetic people, even in the strictest economic sense.

A ship was once docked at a foreign port. After unloading the goods, the ship was supposed to leave. But due to a technical problem, the ship could not start. The engineers did their best, but they could not figure out what the issue was.

Keeping the ship at the same dock was a costly affair. The crew finally decided to call an engineer from their own land, where the ship had originated from. But they figured that getting the engineer to reach the ship would take about three or four days.

A local person suggested contacting a retired engineer who was staying close by and had experience in solving such technical issues. This retired person was immediately called to resolve the problem. Within a short period of time, he figured out the issue and quickly fixed it. The ship was up and running and left the shores soon after.

Had they waited for the foreign engineer to come, their cost would have gone up further. Now the problem got resolved in no time, plus the local engineer did not charge anything at all. This is just one example of retired people not just being cost-effective but also being undervalued. We see them as a liability, while in reality they are an asset.

There are many rules and regulations that Chanakya makes for not just protecting the old people but also giving them special privileges.

In the rules formed by the department of shipping, Chanakya gives them special status too.

> Brahmins, wandering monks, children, old persons, sick persons, carriers of royal edicts and pregnant women should cross with a sealed pass from the controller of shipping. (2.28.18)

In the above sutra we find that the controller of shipping gives the old people and the others mentioned a pass that will allow them to use the services free of cost.

This is almost like the senior citizens card that is being issued by the government. These senior citizens can use the card at various places to get special privileges and discounts. This shows that society really appreciates them and cares for them.

Today, in most public places and facilities like transport, there are seats reserved for senior citizens. There are even special coaches for them to travel.

Let us take another example of Chanakya taking care of old people.

This is a totally different department—the department of courtesans. The superintendent of the courtesans' department (*ganikadhyaksha*) was also supposed to take care of the old women in the profession. Chanakya had made rules where the senior ladies were not just protected but also given an elevated status.

We can see this being indicated in book number two, chapter twenty-seven, sutra number four.

Chanakya says:

In conformity with superiority in point of beauty and ornaments, he should, with one thousand panas, assign the lowest, middlemost or highest turn for attendance, in order to add distinction to attendance with the parasol, the water jug, the fan, the palanquin, the seat and the chariot. In case of loss of beauty, he should appoint her as the 'mother'. (2.27.4)

The work of a person also depends on the age group he or she belongs to. Every person has a certain capacity to work, which is dependent on the body and its aging process. Certain activities can be done only at certain age. For example, heavy physical work becomes impossible to do as we age.

So what did Chanakya do for such people in a profession? He allocated the work according to their ages as well. When the courtesan is young and beautiful, she is given a different salary (thousand *pana*s in this case), and then, according to the work done, he gives them the middle, the lowest or the highest salary.

What happens to those who have become old and have lost their beauty? They are made 'mothers'. In the world of courtesans, beauty matters the most. Physical appearance is a key factor for success in the trade. But as they age, beauty will naturally fade away. So should they be removed from the system and the profession?

No, they are simply elevated in the profession. They are given a promotion instead.

They are made 'mothers'—meaning the overall well-being of the group is now their responsibility. Plus we need to note that these mother courtesans are also paid very well. This is dignity for senior citizens. What they want is to be accepted by the people around them. The best way to show them value is to give them an elevated status in the profession.

The 'mother' is a person who will take care of the whole family. She will know the requirement of each person in the family; she will provide them with their needs. Plus the mother will keep a keen supervisory eye on each person. No one can escape the love and the fear of the mother.

3. Women's Empowerment

Another area where we see the softer side of Chanakya, apart from taking care of old people, is women's empowerment.

Today we talk about women's empowerment and about giving them social status across the globe. Gender equality is the most commonly discussed topic even by national leaders. It is also becoming a matter of policy to appoint women in various positions. Companies have started taking women at leadership levels to make sure they walk their talk.

For Chanakya, women's empowerment was a key factor for social and national development. He would consider women's empowerment from various aspects, right from social status to economic empowerment to educating them. The overall personality development of women was considered very important.

Throughout the *Arthashastra*, we see this being done in many places. From making them a part of the espionage system, and respecting female monks, to giving rights and privileges to courtesans and also legally empowering them, we find that Chanakya treated women with dignity and gave them respectable positions everywhere.

In the administration found in the *Arthashastra* we find an interesting government department that focused on women's development. It dealt both with social and economic aspects. This was the textile industry. The ministers, the government officials as well as the superintendent-in-charge made the textile industry very women-friendly,

Let us look at some key aspects from this part of the *Arthashastra*—book two, chapter twenty-three, section forty is called 'The Superintendent of Yarns and Textiles'.

The whole textile industry consisted of female employees. Even in the modern days, women constitute more than 80 per cent of the workforce of the textile industry. The policies and decisions, therefore, have to be made keeping the women in the centre.

Chanakya starts first by recruiting women from various sectors of the society.

He says:

> He should get yarn spun out of wood, bark-fibres, cotton, silk-cotton, hemp and flax, through widows, crippled women, maidens, women who have left their homes and women paying off their fines by personal labour, through mothers of courtesans, through old female servants of the king and through female servants of temples whose services of the gods have ceased. (2.23.2)

What kinds of women are employed in the textile industry is given above. Let us see a few of them in detail.

Widows: The widows were to be given economic empowerment. Men would be the primary breadwinners of the family. Once the husband dies, there has to be an economic support system. So the first preference of employment is given to widows. They will, in turn, use the money earned to take care of their family.

Crippled women: The worst form of being crippled is not physical but mental. Even though the lady may be crippled, if she is skilled in some craft, she can make a living. She need not be dependent on someone else. Chanakya would identify such ladies and give them skill-development training.

Note that such ladies who could not come to the factory had the option of working from home. The cotton and the raw material would reach them at home and they would make the product in their houses itself.

Women who have left their homes: For various reasons, young girls and women leave homes and land up in cities and other places. Say, a young girl in love with a boy runs away from her family to get married to him. Later she realizes that the boy was a fraud; she does not know what to do. Neither can she go back to her house, nor can she stay on her own in that new place.

For such people, Chanakya made arrangements for social security. He gave them employment and empowered them.

Old female servants of kings: Kings had many servants. This included female servants too. After a point, they have to retire. Like any job, there is a date of retirement, when you leave your seat and give a place for the next generation to take over. But some retired people may still require financial assistance. Maybe there is no other earning member in their family. Or, their children may not be capable of earning. Or there may not be enough savings to take care of themselves in old age. Therefore, an employment guarantee is given to such old servants of the king.

Old female servants of temples: Temples were another space where women were employed. India has seen a full era of 'temple economy'. It was a robust system where many spiritual and economic activities used to take place. The ladies also used to be part of the workforce in temples. Again, when the time for retirement came, they were given alternative employment in the textile industry.

Sexual harassment at the workplace: Chanakya had a deep understanding of society. He was aware that if there were female workers and those in charge at the workplace were men, there was a greater chance of sexual harassment. He had made many strict laws to prevent such harassment.

Women have a sixth sense. They can perceive the intentions behind each look and touch of their male colleagues. If a superior made advances, there were systems to make direct complaints to higher authorities. Very strict action would be taken against the offender, including immediate removal from his job. In extreme cases, capital punishment would be considered.

Thus, inside the mind of Chanakya, we only see respect and the wish to ensure dignity for women. His was a mind that believed that gods reside in places where women are respected.

4. Respect for Teachers

There are different types of teachers and there are different types of students. Chanakya was a rare combination of an excellent teacher and an excellent student.

Therefore, all his students respected him. Chanakya respected all his teachers as well. Right from the beginning of the *Arthashastra* till the end of the book, we find Chanakya admiring his teachers—those who taught the subject of the Arthashastra before him.

The interesting part is that Chanakya does not necessarily agree with all his teachers. But he respects them. There are differences of opinions and views. Yet, there is reverence for them. One does not have to necessarily agree with someone to respect them. Difference of opinion is a strength rather than a weakness.

Let us look at a few sutras that throw light upon this aspect of Chanakya, taking into consideration different views by other acharyas.

Kautilya's *Arthashastra* opens with the following prayers to his teachers:

Om. Namah Sukra Abhyam
Om. Salutations to Shukra and Brihaspati

In our tradition, teachers are respected the most. And we believe in the guru–shishya parampara, where every student becomes a teacher, and every teacher is someone's student. This is the knowledge tradition that we follow.

In the above prayer, we find salutations being offered to two great teachers, Shukra and Brihaspati.

Shukra—the guru of the demons or the rakshasas. He guided his students in warfare and also taught them how to run a kingdom effectively.

Brihaspati—the guru of the gods or the devtas. He was a master strategist himself who taught rajaniti to his students.

An interesting aspect to note is that both would give opposing views to their students as their students were from opposite camps. So there will be multiple and contradictory strategies proposed to achieve victory in war.

Chanakya would come up with a different strategy all together. Instead of supporting one side, it is always better to learn from both sides. A good student does not take sides, nor does he or she compare two teachers. Each teacher has his or her own style and method of teaching. They may even have different theories and value systems as well. But why get into a debate about who is right and who is wrong? It is best to learn from all.

Chanakya further continues:

This single treatise on the Science of Politics has been prepared mostly by bringing together the teachings of as many treatises on the Science of Politics as have been composed by ancient teachers for the acquisition and protection of the earth. (1.1.1)

How Chanakya wrote his own *Arthashastra* has been described in this sutra. He says that this single treatise was prepared by bringing together the teachings of various gurus.

Chanakya studied the previous teachers of the Arthashastra. This indicates that Kautilya's *Arthashastra* is not the first or the only Arthashastra—there were many before his.

Chanakya had studied many experts in the science of politics. Kautilya's *Arthashastra* mentions fourteen such teachers who were masters in the field of political thought.

Chanakya also informs us about the reason for writing his own Arthashastra. It was meant for the acquisition and protection of the earth. The objective was clear from the very beginning—meaning, he wanted to conquer the whole world, not by killing, but through various other strategies.

Similarly, in any subject, a good student should learn from multiple teachers and also respect the difference of opinion. From that will come knowledge and wisdom. And through the experiences and theories of other teachers, one can build a theory oneself. The *Arthashastra* by Chanakya is an example.

Let us see a few incidents in the life of Chanakya where he made sure that he was a winner, yet had a soft corner for the enemy as well.

5. Letting Go of the Enemy

Alexander was a ruthless conqueror. He wanted to win over the whole world. He had come from Greece, where his teacher was the great philosopher Aristotle.

When Alexander left on his mission, his teacher had told him to bring back from India something he would not get anywhere else—spirituality. So, Alexander knew that India was not rich just on the outside but also on the inside.

When he reached the frontiers of India, he was defeated by Chanakya and his strategies. This came as a shock for the king who had never before lost a battle. His army was demoralized and, unable to face the unfamiliar Indian conditions, Alexander had to turn back.

The interesting part is that Chanakya had the full power not only to defeat Alexander but also to kill him. But he chose to avoid it. After all, Chanakya's objective was victory, not the death of his enemy.

On his way back to Greece, Alexander died. However, two things were always on Chanakya's mind: First, even if Alexander was dead, his army could come back to attack again. Second, Alexander came from Greece, another great civilization of that time. Chanakya did not want to miss out on an opportunity to learn from them. So, he tried to come up with a strategy to solve both matters simultaneously.

The general of Alexander's army was Seleucus. Chanakya got his student and king Chandragupta married to Seleucus's daughter, Helen. By doing this, he achieved the results he wanted. The enemy would now never think of another attack. After all, the queen was one of them.

Next, Chanakya knew that when a lady marries into a house, she brings not just herself but also her culture along. She can transform her husband's house with this knowledge.

And so we see that Chanakya had a soft spot for the Greeks. He did not want to kill the enemy, but the enmity itself.

He used the same principle while defeating Dhanananda, the last king of the Nanda dynasty. Dhanananda was a tyrant. He had even killed Chanakya's father, who used to advise him on good governance. Unfortunately, Dhanananda showed no signs of reforming.

Chanakya changed tack, and with the help of his students, led by Chandragupta, defeated Dhanananda. Chanakya could have easily killed him. But, like he did with Alexander, he left him alive. Dhanananda was exiled to the forest. There was, however, a difference.

While Alexander died a natural death, Dhanananda was still alive. There was a good chance that he would come back and attack. It would not have been difficult for the ousted king to gather support in his kingdom.

A person asked Chanakya, 'Acharya, you have let Dhanananda go; what if he comes back to destroy us?'

With a crooked smile, Chanakya answered, 'One should let the enemy go in such a way that he never comes back.' And after a pause, he continued, 'But never trust the enemy. Forgive but do not forget. My spies are keeping an eye on him even in the forest. Everything that Dhanananda does is under my control.'

This was another side of Chanakya: soft-hearted and focused at the same time. This, also, is aanvikshiki.

7

Chanakya's Thoughts on Management

We have been discussing and learning about the various kinds of thoughts that went inside the mind of Chanakya. But in this chapter, we shall try to take a different approach.

We will start by imagining him in the present generation.

What if the fourth-century-BC Chanakya were to come to the twenty-first century? What would he do? Would he try to change nations the way he did before? Would he try and manage the economics of the state very differently than what he did in his generation?

Would he handle people differently? Would his advice be different to the current generation? Would he still want to create a king like Chandragupta Maurya? Would the leadership education that he might give to leaders change in any manner?

Would technology play a major part in his systems? Would satellites replace his information-gathering mechanisms? How would he look at democracy as a method of election over a monarchical system?

How would trade be different between interconnected nations? Would speed of travel and communication make any difference in his approach while dealing with human relationships?

There could be many such questions to think about.

In all the formats of governance, he would surely see one more striking difference—in the way wealth is being created in this generation. It is getting more organized and systematic. Today, companies are wealth creators. The tax structures have changed. It is now all about corporate culture. The kings have become business families.

Thus, in the present day, Chanakya would have to look into 'corporate management theories' and become what could be called the Corporate Chanakya.

In the current corporate and management scenario, we find a lack of business ethics. The basic framework of corporate governance that modern corporations have designed remains confined to paper. There's hardly any practical application. And this is a serious issue, especially because the corporates are the prime movers in society. So let's delve deep into the philosophy of the world's first management guru, Chanakya.

Chanakya's Research Methodology

Management is now considered a science. There is a lot of research taking place in the field of management. So how would Chanakya have gone about with his management research?

He would study the books written by management experts—in the same vein that he referred to gurus like

Shukra and Brihaspati while writing the *Arthashastra*. He would make notes and compare the different theories of management scientists. Critically and with due respect, he would evaluate these theories. Only then would he arrive at his 'own truth' and do the right and the necessary.

He would then bring out an updated edition of the *Arthashastra* for this generation. And it would deal with both the conceptual and application levels.

He would also conduct a peer review of his findings, thereby asserting that his theories are not a figment of the imagination, but rooted in the science of management. Also, he would consult the entire gamut of leadership—political, military, bureaucratic and corporate. This is a foolproof way of testing a new theory.

Today, one of the challenges in India is the judicial system. It cries out for a lot of management applications since justice delayed is justice denied. The entire process of arriving at a good and sound judgement is time-consuming and sometimes, even a fair trial is missing.

Chanakya, clearly, would solve the crisis that our judicial system is facing and ensure that no culprit goes unpunished.

The field of management, as that of rajaniti (politics), includes all fields. A corporate leader or a politician should be equipped with all-round knowledge. She or he should be well versed in all the disciplines. Now let us take a look at all the areas that Kautilya covered in his *Arthashastra*.

Kautilya's *Arthashastra*

We find the roots of the *Arthashastra* in the Rig Veda. The *Arthashastra* deals primarily with economics, politics (statecraft) and punishment (dandaniti). It is a treatise based on pure logic.

The *Arthashastra* contains 6000 sutras, fifteen books, 150 chapters and 180 sections. The fifteen books can be classified thus: book one is on the fundamentals of management; book two deals with economics; books three, four and five are on law; books six, seven and eight describe foreign policies; books nine to fourteen concern subjects of war; and the fifteenth book deals with the methodology and devices used in writing the *Arthashastra*.

However, it also needs to be stated that these are general classifications. We can learn of areas covered in one book from other books too. For example, we can learn about the fundamentals of management from not only book one but also from books two, eight and ten.

Also, various specialized sciences are described in the *Arthashastra*, including gemmology, Ayurveda and architecture. And in this process, we get an insider's view into the mastermind of Kautilya.

Another interesting revelation is that Kautilya's *Arthashastra* is not the first of its kind. From a number of quotations and references in later works, we come to know that there were at least four distinct schools and thirteen individual teachers of the Arthashastra before Kautilya. Throughout his work, he refers to various acharyas, which include Bharadvaja, Visalaksa, Parasara, Pisuna and Kaunapadanta. It may have to do with the practicality of Kautilya's *Arthashastra* that other such works got lost with the passage of time.

The very reason that this book has come down to our generation after nearly 2400 years shows us that he had really fine-tuned each concept. That's the farsightedness of Kautilya who delved into human psychology that never changes with time.

Kautilya wrote this landmark treatise for his disciple king, Chandragupta Maurya. In this chapter, we shall limit ourselves to the management aspects delineated in the *Arthashastra*.

All about Management

Book one, titled *Vinayadhikarikam* ('Concerning the Topic of Training'), deals with training, and lays out the fundamentals of management. It has 500 sutras spread over twenty-one chapters and eighteen sections. The book starts by defining the areas that are going to be covered. This is done by giving a basic structure of the *Arthashastra*, starting with the enumeration of the sections and books as also the sciences (chapters one to four).

As for that most important aspect of training, unlike the current way of learning in a business school, Kautilya believed in the guru–shishya parampara. Hence, chapter five is titled 'Association with Elders'. It's very important for us to understand at this point that any knowledge that we need to gather ought not to be merely theory-based. The emphasis has to be on practicality and mentorship.

Chanakya has also been generally criticized by many who have compared him to Machiavelli, the author of *The Prince*, which contains methods that could seem *adharmic* or unrighteous. However, this comparison may not be justified, as Kautilya puts a lot of stress on self-control and on the proper methods of winning over the enemy. Chapter six, titled

'Control over the Senses', brings out a totally different aspect of Kautilya, which many current interpretations of the work generally miss. In this chapter, he elaborates through twelve sutras the importance of control over the senses; that is, how to give up *kama* (lust), *krodha* (anger), *lobha* (greed), *mana* (pride), *mada* (arrogance) and *harsha* (foolhardiness). He gives various examples of kings who perished, having overindulged the senses. Finally, in the twelfth sutra, he concludes by quoting King Jamdagnya and Amarisa, two kings who enjoyed the earth for a long time, having controlled their senses. Therefore, the first teaching of Kautilya urges you 'to conquer the internal enemies before you conquer the external enemies'.

All management starts with self-management, says Chanakya.

This idea is further discussed in chapter seven, with section three covering the topic of the 'Sage King'. The king wields control by weeding out the six enemies of the senses; he cultivates his intellect by association with elders; keeps a watchful eye by means of spies; brings about security and well-being by (energetic) activity; maintains the observance of special duties by the subjects by carrying out his own duties; acquires discipline by receiving instruction in the sciences; attains popularity by knowing what is of material advantage; and maintains proper behaviour by doing what is beneficial. (1.7.1)

Here we come to note that for Kautilya, the 'Sage King' is the ideal. He has clearly set in front of us what is expected out of an ideal king by describing him in the very beginning itself.

Among the three purusharthas of dharma, artha and kama, Kautilya gives top priority to artha. 'Material well-being alone is supreme,' he says, for spiritual good and sensual pleasures depend on material well-being (1.7.6–7). This makes Kautilya different from very many other thinkers. That is why the book is rightly named the *Arthashastra*. This may seem a bit confusing to the novices, especially those with a religious background. Hence, Kautilya's *Arthashastra* is addressed to rulers in particular and not to the common man.

This is not a *dharmashastra* but an Arthashastra. Kautilya says the primary responsibility of a king is to maintain the material and physical well-being of his subjects. Having a strong material foundation (artha) will render kama and dharma easy to achieve.

The appointment of amatyas (persons who are close to the king) is the next important aspect of management, says Chanakya (1.8). This is followed by the appointment of the *mantri* and the *purohit*, that is, minister and chaplain. The duties of all three are to advise the king on various matters and be with him through thick and thin. Hence, their selection process is carefully considered. This is done by ascertainment of their integrity by means of secret tests (1.10). It also suggests various tests for ensuring their faithfulness to the king.

We can directly relate this to today's corporate world where the selection and appointment of managers is a carefully planned process. Today, HR departments play a key role in the recruitment of able managers. Kautilya proceeds with the creation of an intelligence network as the next management process. The appointment of persons in the secret service and the creation of an establishment of spies are considered in detail in section seven. He suggests the recruitment of the following categories of people in the secret service: sharp pupil, the apostate monk, the supposed householder, trader, ascetic, a braveheart, a poison giver and a begging nun (1.11.1). He also lays down the rules for the secret servants in section eight. These spies and secret agents are then set to keep a watch on the citizens. They have to monitor the seducible and the non-seducible parties in their territory (section nine). Then there's a discussion on how to win over the seducible and non-seducible parties in the enemy territory (section ten).

Section eleven deals with counsel. A king is advised not to take any decision without the help of consultation. And this consultation should be done in secrecy (1.15.3). The affairs of a king are threefold—namely., directly perceived, unperceived and inferred (1.15.19). Therefore, he should sit in counsel with those who are mature in intellect. 'All undertakings should be preceded by consultation. Holding a consultation with only one, he may not be able to reach a decision in difficult matters. With more councillors it is difficult to reach decisions and maintain secrecy,' says Kautilya (1.15.2, 35, 40). He advises that a king should despise none, should listen to the opinion of everyone and should pay heed to even a child's wise counsel (1.15.22).

Section twelve states the rules for the envoy; how he should pass on the message to the enemy and protect himself while in their territory.

The leader of any organization, says Kautilya, should be able to maintain high standards:

'If the king is energetic, his subjects will be equally energetic. If he is slack (and lazy in performing his duties) the subjects will also be lazy, [and] thereby, eat into his wealth. Besides, a lazy king will easily fall into the hands of the enemies. Hence the king should himself always be energetic.' (1.19.1–5) And inspirational too.

Then he moves on to the time management principles that a king should follow (1.19.7–25). He should be able to maintain an open-door policy and attend to affairs of holy places, hermitages, heretics, Brahmins learned in the Vedas, cattle and holy places, minors, the aged, the sick, the distressed and the helpless and women (1.19.26–29). The root of material well-being is activity, says Chanakya, while the opposite behaviour brings material disaster; in the absence of activity, there is certain destruction of what is obtained and of what is not yet received. Activity ensures rich rewards (1.19.35–36).

Having established the characteristics of a good king, book two, *Adhyakshaprachara* (The Activity of Heads of Departments), deals with economics. Consisting of thirty-six chapters, it describes in detail all that is required for the proper functioning of an economy. Some of the topics pursued are: setting up of revenue collection, records, accounts and audit offices; starting of mines and factories; settlement of the countryside; construction of forts; the appointment and responsibilities of various departmental heads; and the inspection of officers. Agriculture, cattle-rearing and trade constitute the main economic activities. The basic traits of a good economy are: acquisition of things not possessed; the preservation of things possessed; and the increase of things owned and the bestowal of them on a worthy recipient. On such factors depend the orderly maintenance of worldly life (1.4.1–4).

The next three books—three, four and five—deal with the legal aspects of running a kingdom. They involve issues concerning judges, valid and invalid transactions, filing of law-suits, non-payment of debts and undertakings in partnerships. This part also deals with how criminals can be brought to book and how secret agents are to be used to detect them. Besides, it dwells on keeping a watch over the crime levels, and also on matters of punishment and investigation.

Books six, seven and eight cover the area of foreign policy. They talk about the importance of a vibrant foreign policy, and spells out categories of kings, such as the neighbouring king, the middle king, neutral king, ally king; and goes on to discuss their strategies. This section is particularly useful in dealing with the economic market in today's highly competitive world.

Then we come to the topic of war in books nine to fourteen. War, says Kautilya, is always the last option. However, when it becomes unavoidable, the preparation of the army becomes essential; he goes on to focus on the right moves in the battlefield and warfare strategies—all of this with extraordinary precision.

Towards the end, we find an astonishing revelation. In section 176, Kautilya deals with the topic of 'pacification of the conquered territory'. He gives due respect to the citizens of the conquered territory and urges that they be treated with honour. After gaining a new territory, the king ought to blank out the enemy's faults with his own virtues and doubly so. He should carry out what is agreeable and beneficial to the subjects by doing his own duty as laid down, granting favours, giving exemptions, presenting gifts and maintaining honour. And he should cause the enemy's seducible party to be favoured as promised; all the more so if they had exerted themselves. He also lays much in store by the king's ability to keep promises; if the king can't do so, he is unworthy of trust. And his behaviour should be akin to that of the subjects. Hence, he should adopt a similar character, dress, language and behaviour as the subjects. He should further show the same devotion in festivals in honour of the deities of the country, festive gatherings and sportive amusements as do his subjects (13.5.3–8). He should cause the honouring of all deities and hermitages, and make grants of land, money and exemptions to men distinguished in learning, speech and piety. He should also order the release of prisoners and render help to the distressed, the helpless and the diseased (13.5.11).

The fifteenth and last book deals with the methodology used in the *Arthashastra*.

Management Findings from Chanakya

Kautilya's *Arthashastra* is a book of pure logic and does not take into account any religious aspect. It deals with the various subjects directly and with razor-like sharpness. Analysed carefully, we find that there are many concepts of the *Arthashastra* which are still applicable in today's corporate world. Kautilya deals with certain principles of management that are eternal and do not change with time. Management is not just an academic subject but a 'mindset' that is carefully developed by control over the senses, association with elders, proper training and guidance, and an overall purpose of the higher good of the society.

A deeper study of the book will open out new areas unknown to the present-day generation.

Now, let's look into one more aspect of management: planning.

Management experts say, 'If you fail to plan, you plan to fail.'

So we will see how Chanakya planned everything in detail.

Town Planning and Public Administration

These principles and strategies of town planning and administration were studied, applied and practised by rulers for many centuries, including by Chandragupta Maurya, Ashoka and Shivaji.

Here we will throw light on a few areas of town planning, public facilities and maintenance of law and order as is applicable in today's world. Public services management is the crux of good governance.

The central theme of Kautilya's *Arthashastra* is: *'Prajasukhe sukham raja, prajacha hite hitam . . .'* ('In the happiness of the subjects lies the benefit of the king and in what is beneficial to the subjects is his own benefit'). (1.19.34)

Kautilya believed that good governance comes from understanding the welfare of the citizens. Kings are advised to take into consideration this aspect before they get into any decision-making process. In the well-being of the citizens and in their happiness lie the benefit and the happiness of the ruler, advises Kautilya.

Below are a few areas that may be beneficial to NGOs, social workers, public servants and decision-makers.

1. New Settlements

Kautilya visualizes the expansion of the state into new settlements and makes provisions to help the people settle in these places, while also facilitating financial support. He says: 'He [the king/ruler] should favour them with grains, cattle and money. These they should pay back afterwards at their convenience.' (2.1.13–14)

Application in today's scenario

Today, every town is getting overcrowded due to rapid population growth. The government should make policies and strategies either to encourage reverse migration to villages or look out for new land where the population can stay, rather than getting concentrated in one place. In order to encourage them, they should be provided with the basic raw materials needed to start new industries, which should be given at low interest rates, tax benefits and easy repayment schemes.

2. Provision of Water

Water is life. All living creatures depend on water. Hence the settlement of people is directly connected with the availability of water. Hence Kautilya recommends: 'Storage reservoirs are to be built using natural springs or water brought from elsewhere.' (2.1.20)

Application in today's scenario

In today's scenario, the wastage of water should be totally prevented. Schemes like rain-water harvesting and building of public water reservoirs should be implemented. Especially in the rainy season, plans should be made at the local level to store water for the whole year. The public should be made aware of the need for controlling water wastage.

3. Building Roads

Roads are the lifeline of any nation. Building of roads and connecting the same to the remotest corner, as also maintaining their beauty, are of prime importance to Kautilya: 'The king was also to help people volunteering to build reservoirs by giving them land, building roads, or by giving them grants of timber and other implements.' (2.1.21)

The king was also supposed to directly help the people get better road connectivity by providing them the required raw materials for this purpose.

Application in today's scenario

The government should give emphasis on building and maintaining good roads. We see that such public property is misused by hawkers in a big way. The local authorities have to take strict action against such persons. The public too has to pitch in for this purpose, as Chanakya would have it.

4. Voluntary Services

Kautilya specifically states that people should obey the orders of anyone who carries out an activity that's welfare-oriented. Good local leaders who voluntarily start new projects and initiatives have to be encouraged. Says Kautilya: 'They shall obey the orders of one who proposes what is beneficial to all.' (3.10.39)

Application in today's scenario

Youngsters should be encouraged to take active interest in the preservation of public places and utilities. They should be trained and imparted the necessary powers to take corrective actions at the local level. More and more volunteers should be called forward to take such initiatives under the guidance of able local leaders.

5. Consumer Protection

Consumer protection is another area that receives elaborate treatment from Kautilya. He says that preventive action needs to be taken against black marketing, adulteration and manipulation of the market.

According to him, 'The king should prevent thieves and thieves such as traders, artisans, actors, mendicants, jugglers and others from oppressing the country.' (4.1.65) He also prescribes fines for cheating the consumer. (4.1.28)

Application in today's scenario

There are all kinds of thieves and thievery operating in the present-day world. Regular thieves who indulge in robbery; then dishonest traders (who sell goods above the prescribed MRP), artisans (who overcharge customers), mendicants (who cheat the public in the name of superstition) and gamblers.

All of them should be stopped. Usually, these kinds of people have a direct or indirect connection with the enemies of the country. So, in order to protect the country, strict action should be taken against them.

6. Crisis Management

Crisis management is another area that Kautilya excelled at, especially during natural calamities. These are some of the steps he suggests: 'Distribution of food at concessional rates to the public, seeking the help of friendly kings, shifting the people to the neighbourhood, migration, and additional cultivation to cope with the emergency.' (4.3.17–20)

Application in today's scenario

Whenever any natural calamity (like floods or earthquakes) occurs, everyone has to immediately get into action. Support from the neighbouring places should be sought. If necessary, the public should be shifted to safer environs. It's imperative that the relief work is carried out as quickly as possible.

7. Civic Amenities and Common Facilities

A lot of emphasis has been laid on providing and protecting public amenities in the *Arthashastra*. Says Kautilya: 'Shades, courtyards, latrines, fireplaces, places for pounding grain and open spaces are to be used as common properties.' (3.8.28)

Application in today's scenario

The common public needs to be provided with public amenities and facilities like shades, natural surroundings, latrines, warm places and open areas like playground and gardens in order to have better health and hygienic conditions for one and all.

8. Attending to Public Problems

Kautilya explicitly states that a king should be accessible to his petitioners and should not make them wait for the redressal of their genuine grievances. 'He [the leader] should allow unrestricted entrance to those wishing to see him in connection with their affairs.' (1.19.26)

Application in today's scenario

Government servants and public administrators need to have an open-door policy. Many key decisions get delayed either due to wrong information or lack of it. This can be solved by letting people come and express their problems directly to the authorities concerned. This will help people feel more safe and comfortable while dealing with government officials.

9. Regular Inspection

No rule can be effective if regular inspections are not conducted and reports are not monitored. Hence Kautilya suggests: 'He [the leader] should constantly hold an inspection of their works, men being inconstant in their minds.' (2.9.2–3)

Application in today's scenario

It is quite natural for a person to slip into complacency if the boss does not conduct regular inspections. Over a period of time, the work tends to be taken for granted. Hence, strict daily and hourly productivity records have to be maintained. A good MIS has to be in place. Only then can systems run smoothly and efficiently.

10. Art of Punishment

Another name for Kautilya's *Arthashastra* is *Dandaniti*, meaning the Art of Punishment. He says: 'If the rod is not used at all, the stronger swallows the weak . . .' (1.4.13–14) And, 'The king severe with the rod [punishment] becomes a terror. A king with a mild rod is despised. The king just with a rod is honoured.' (1.4.8–10)

Application in today's scenario

If strict action is not taken, the law of the jungle will prevail in any place. However, the leader should not become a tyrant. At the same time, he should not become too soft. The punishment should be just and balanced. Such a punishment and punisher is always respected. Only if punishment is carried out will there be seriousness in the conduct of work. If not, slowly, corruption will set into the whole system.

An Overview of Chanakya and Management

The management principles in the *Arthashastra* are eternal in its relevance. Many things change, but Chanakya's focus is on the timeless.

Management is all about managing the minds of the people. First, the leader has to manage himself, then by the use of many tools and techniques, he has to manage others.

Our country can once again use this text as a road map to rebuild an Indian management theory that would spell success for this present generation. We are now talking about smart cities, model towns and villages that would provide every citizen with the basic necessities of life. This should be supported by an effective law and order machinery. It will help each individual feel safe and secure, and also contribute to the nation-building process.

When such strong and effective management principles are used, not just companies, institutions and organizations, but a whole nation can evolve into the next level of productivity and effectiveness.

8

The Duties of a King

Chanakya did not think only of himself, he thought about the king and his duties as well. He went to the extent of creating an extensive categorization of the duties for a king on a daily basis. This gave the king a sort of to-do list to follow. A minute-to-minute routine was set up by Chanakya.

The Daily Routine of a King

The king, according to Kautilya, is supposed to live a very active and austere life. He is an ascetic in the true sense. Therefore, the ideal is of a rajarishi. This life of a sage-like king has been dealt with in detail throughout the *Arthashastra*, and the training is outlined for him accordingly.

The brilliance of any teacher comes from the fact that they look at all dimensions of their knowledge, from concept to application. Theory being put into practice is the best form of knowledge implementation.

Kautilya also makes sure that while detailing the daily routine of a king, a continuous active life is outlined. When the king is active, the subjects become active, following his example.

The king has to set an example. It is always a top-down approach. One has to walk the talk and lead by example. When the king is lethargic, the subjects will, in turn, become lethargic. An active leader can make an inactive person active. And active followers can become lethargic if the king demonstrates lethargy. And this leads to corrupt practices among the subjects and the government officials. Moreover, he is overreached by enemies, presenting an opportunity to his opponents who are waiting for a chance to take over the kingdom. Therefore, the king should be active.

Division of the Day and Night

To keep the king active day and night, a routine has been prescribed. The day is divided into eight parts and the night into eight parts by means of *nalika*s.

A nalika is a unit of time equal to ninety minutes. Thus, twenty-four hours are divided into sixteen parts of ninety minutes each, eight during the day and eight during the night.

A shadow measuring three *paurusa*s, one paurusa (and) four *angula*s, and the midday when the shadow disappears, these are the four earlier eighth part of the day. Similarly are explained the later four parts.

Out of them, during the first eighth of the day, he should listen to measures taken for defence and (accounts of) income and expenditure. During the second, he should look into the affairs of his subjects. During the third, he should take his bath and his meals and devote himself to study. During the fourth, he should receive revenue in cash and assign tasks to heads of departments. During the fifth, he should consult the council of ministers by sending letters, and acquaint himself with the information brought in by spies. During the sixth, he should engage in recreation or hold consultations. During the seventh, he should review elephants, horses, chariots and troops. During the eighth, he should deliberate on military plans with the commander-in-chief.

When the day is ended, he should worship the evening twilight.

During the first eighth of the night, he should interview secret agents. During the second, he should take a bath, eat his meals and engage in study. During the third, he should go to bed to the strains of music and sleep during the fourth and the fifth parts. During the sixth, he should awaken to the sounds of musical instruments and ponder over the teachings of the science of politics as well as over the work to be done. During the seventh, he should sit in consultation (with councillors) and dispatch secret agents.

During the eighth, he should receive blessings from priests and preceptors, and see his physician, chief cook and astrologer. And after going around a cow with her calf and a bull, he should proceed to the assembly hall.

Understanding the Daily Routine

An analysis of this daily routine of a king gives us interesting insights into how Kautilya had planned an overall development of the king's personality. The routine touches all aspects of his overall development: physical, mental, intellectual and spiritual. It is a very dynamic structure, yet gives immense time for study, recreation, the practice of aanvikshiki (thinking time), sleep, consultation, exercise and travel.

Sleep

Dividing the twenty-four hours into units of one and half hours each, the king is supposed to wake up at 1.30 a.m. in the night. One may wonder why, when most of our generation would sleep at that time, such an early wake-up time is suggested? Now this also does not mean his sleep is not complete.

The king is advised to sleep early, at about 9 p.m. He sleeps for four and half hours in the night. It is supplemented with an additional one and a half hours in the afternoon.

Thus, a total of six hours of sleep is suggested in a day, which is the duration of sleep recommended for any active and healthy person.

However, in the afternoon, the king is given a choice between taking a full nap and taking part in recreations, pleasure activities or even consultations. Even today, power naps are encouraged for working professionals, giving them a much-needed break on a hectic day.

But if he does not feel sleepy in the afternoon, instead of forcing himself to take a power nap, some recreational activities like games, meditation or even having a conversation with some experts are suggested; the decision is left to the king.

While going to sleep, he has to listen to music, and he must also awaken to the sound of musical instruments, suggested Kautilya. Music has a way of getting us to relax at a subconscious level and also develops fineness of thinking, important for a king to develop a subtle intellect, which is, in turn, crucial for decision-making. Also, music has got a therapeutic value, according to mental health researchers, even to the level of helping us have pleasant, peaceful dreams instead of nightmares.

Wake-up Activity

The mind starts its thought activities the moment a person rises from sleep. Either these thoughts can be directed towards useful purposes or the mental energy can be completely drained away. Providing the right direction to early-morning thoughts will make the day productive and the king efficient.

'Ponder over the teachings of the science of politics'—this is to be done. The king has learnt the science of politics, dandaniti, and right thinking, aanvikshiki, during his training. However, practice on a daily basis is important.

During the previous day, he may have encountered various situations, issues and challenges which require deliberation and deep thinking before further action. So this is the right time for considering them and rethinking them, using the knowledge from the scriptures he has learnt like the trais, Atharva Veda and Itihasa Veda.

Looking into the past and getting guidance from the suggestions and the wisdom of the scriptures, and the past experiences of previous teachers and historical events, helps the king to tackle any situation with ease.

Thinking Time

During this thinking time (aanvikshiki), he is to think over work to be done. Plan out your work and work out your plan. Thus, careful planning for the day ahead results in better scheduling and optimum productivity. If one does not plan the day in advance, it is quite possible that one may get carried away by the demands of others.

Consulting

The next nalika, of one and half hours, from 3 a.m. to 4.30 a.m., is meant for sitting and consulting with councillors, as well as dispatching secret agents. Once the king has carefully planned his day on his own, he goes to get expert advice.

The timing of these meetings indicates that the king and his advisers were ready for the day much before dawn. When the king and his think tank are hard at work day and night, naturally the rest of the government will work towards the welfare of the kingdom and its subjects—that is, for *praja sukhe*.

The *mantriparishad*, the team of experts, will guide the king and provide the inputs needed for decision-making. This is also the time when they give him the daily updates on the activities of various departments.

Each mantri or amatya, along with the raja purohit, would provide solutions to various problems. Consulting with his councillors helps the king broaden his perspective.

Time with Secret Agents

At the same time as the consultations with his experts, the king would dispatch secret agents.

Secret agents are an important part of the king's information network. A whole book, *Kantakashodhana*, containing thirteen chapters and 418 sutras are devoted by Kautilya to this subject. Also, throughout the *Arthashastra* there are references to secret agents and their network, as well as various activities prescribed to them.

This robust intelligence network is active day and night, both inside and outside the kingdom. The objective is to establish control and eliminate crime and criminals. The agents posted within the kingdom gather information about all sorts of criminal activities in the country.

While Kautilya uses these secret agents to monitor the masses, he also keeps an eye on his own men, in order to detect the misappropriation of revenue by officers, for example, and subsequently, recover what was taken.

He also uses the secret agents to gather information on neighbouring kings, enemy kings and various kingdoms in the *rajamandala*.

These secret agents were given an array of powers: they could arrest people based on suspicion, carry out investigations using interrogation and torture, keep a watch over various government departments and mete out punishment for transgressions, including the infliction of secret punishment. Additionally, they were trained to utilize strategies such as sama, dana, bheda and danda.

However, to ensure that the secret agents do not misuse their powers, a system of counter-spying was also created.

Kautilya, while giving a formal structure to the institution of spying, made sure that there was a regular review and monitoring of the system as part of the daily routine of the king.

'Coming to know what is known, definite strengthening of what has become known, removal of doubt in case of two possible alternatives, finding out the rest in a matter that is partly known—this can be achieved by external sources (secret agents).'

This system of the king receiving daily reports from the intelligence services is still practised in our times. The chief minister of a state has a daily morning review with the director general of police, the president meets with the heads of the three armed forces (the President of India being the supreme commander of the military), and the prime minister consults with his national security adviser.

Spiritual Activities

Once the analysis of crime is done and actions are put in motion to counter it, along with the mapping of external threats, the king is free to focus on his daily religious rituals. He is supposed to go to seek the blessings of various people for the day. These include the priest (*ritvik*), preceptors (*raja guru* and teachers) and chaplain (raja purohit). Our Indian culture teaches us to take the blessings of our parents, grandparents and other elders on a daily basis.

Rituals have their own scientific and psychological bases. In the introduction to his book *Indian Culture: Why Do We . . . ?* Swami Chinmayananda explains the logic behind customs and rituals (*aachaar*s). He says the Bhagavadgita defines *Sanaathana dharma* thus: 'Sanaathana' (eternal) means that which cannot be destroyed by fire, weapons, water, air, and which is present in all living and non-living beings. 'Dharma' refers to the way of life which is the 'total of all aachaars'. Sanaathana dharma has its foundation in scientific spirituality. In ancient Hindu literature, we can see that science and spirituality are integrated. It is mentioned in the fortieth chapter of the Yajur Veda, titled 'Isaavaasya Upanishad', that one must use scientific knowledge for solving problems in one's life and must use spiritual knowledge for attaining immortality through a philosophical outlook.

In India, everyone followed aachaars for their above-mentioned benefits: psychological, physiological, familial, social and nationalistic. It is our right and duty to understand scientifically, rationally and logically the meaning of each and every aachaar and follow the same in our lives systematically.

Time with Physician, Cook and Astrologer

After completing the customary rituals, Kautilya advises the king to see his physician. The king's physician was not like the modern-day doctor. The physician would have knowledge of the herbs and medicines and the various diseases that would occur during seasonal changes; solutions were customized for every patient.

This *vaidya* would be an expert in Ayurveda, which includes treatments for both the body and the mind. A daily health check-up would ensure the holistic well-being of the person. This close monitoring ensures a long and healthy life.

Next he meets the chief cook. This too is a daily round to the kitchen. He takes a look at the kind of foodgrains and activities in the kitchen. A discussion with the cook gives him an idea of the seasonal foods available in the kingdom. Any shortfall can be easily taken care of. He can also suggest any special dishes that he wishes to be prepared.

The king also meets the astrologer (*jyotishi*). Chanakya, himself an expert in astrology and suggesting that the same be studied by kings during their training, knew the value of the science of astrology. Astrology, along with astronomy, is used by Chanakya for various activities of the kingdom; for instance, to predict seasonal changes for better farming and irrigation activities, to plan for war and also for daily planning and forecasting.

It is to be noted that astrology should not be used just for future predictions but for future creation. It is a double-edged sword and Chanakya has gone to the extent of even warning the king against total dependency on the stars and planetary positioning to take decisions: 'Wealth will slip away from the foolish person who continuously consults the stars; for wealth is the star of wealth; what will the stars do? Capable men will certainly secure wealth at least after a hundred trials.'

The study and knowledge of astrology should become our guiding force and strength rather than becoming a weakness and mental trap. Therefore, it is also suggested as *guhya vidya* (secret knowledge) in the book of secret conduct.

One more daily ritual suggested for the king is to go round a cow with her calf and a bull. The cow has been considered sacred in the Indian tradition and has been given the status of a mother (*gau-mata*).

Time with Praja

With all these preparations after four and half hours from the time he wakes up, the king is now ready to take up his public role and proceeds to the assembly hall.

Steven Covey, in his book, *Seven Habits of Highly Effective People*, states that private victory is to be achieved before public victory. Private victory refers to mastering the self, and public victory refers to mastering relationships with others. The important note is that private victory must always precede public victory.

This is also called the inside-out approach to life. You must look inside yourself first, develop yourself and clear the limiting factors in your own life, before you become effective in your public life. This makes so much sense and is the best way to succeed in the long run—only if you truly master yourself can you be effective and even lead others.

Thus equipped with spiritual power, the blessings of wise people, information about his kingdom and ideas gleaned from discussions with experts, the king is ready to meet his *praja*, his own people.

Arriving in the assembly hall, he should allow unrestricted entrance to those wishing to see him in connection with their affairs. The king should be easily accessible. That is, one should not need any prior appointment.

This practice is important for any leader. Once the gap between the leader and the followers is minimized, there will be transparency in the system. There is always the danger of the king's men becoming stronger than the king and misusing their powers if the people do not have direct access to their ruler. Even amatyas and mantris can be kept in check through this process.

A king difficult to access is made to do the reverse of what ought to be done, and what ought not to be done, by those near him. Thus an open forum ensures that both the king and the king's men are doing their respective duties. This kind of *jana-sabha* is followed by successful leaders in politics even today.

Being a public representative, the leader should be able to address the people's problems directly. As a consequence, he may face an insurrection of the subjects or subjugation by the enemy.

Affairs of the People

What kinds of affairs did the people discuss with the king?

He should look into the affairs of temple deities, hermitages, heretics, Brahmins learned in the Vedas, cattle and holy places, of minors, the aged, the sick, the distressed and the helpless and of women.

The affairs cover a wide range and spectrum of the society, right from the learned Brahmins, who would have spiritual discussions, to the challenges of various hermitages and temple deities. Chanakya is concerned about the well-being of the poor and the helpless and those who are totally facing bad luck and are in distress. Even women, children (minors) and senior citizens (aged) are taken care of by the king as his own family. And in all cases, the king should favour the stricken (subjects) like a father, asserts Kautilya.

An important point to note is the mention of heretics in the open assembly. Heretics refers to those who believe or teach something that goes against accepted or official beliefs, those who hold unorthodox beliefs in any field. These people could openly challenge any decision or belief of the king or the existing system. His mention of them shows the democratic attitude of the king. If someone challenges a king openly, those opinions too have to be respected in a democracy. Thus we find that democratic monarchy was prescribed by Kautilya when he suggested the formation of a rajarishi.

Priority of Work

In an open public meeting, there is always a chance that one case or issue might take more time than expected. Therefore, the king should prioritize, consider matters in the order of urgency and then take the appropriate decision in every matter.

He should hear every urgent matter immediately, and not put it off. With the kind of administrative responsibilities a leader has, it is important to clear matters as soon as they come up. If work is kept pending, the matters gets piled up to the extent that one will be totally lost and all things will get clogged up.

The famous Kabir *doha* (couplet) makes up this point, *kal kare so aaj kar, aaj kare so ab, pal mein pralaya hoyegi, bahuri karoge kab*. Do tomorrow's work today, today's work anon, if the moment is lost, when will the work be done?

Decision-making

Kautilya also explains how the king should take decisions related to wise people. He suggests adopting extreme respect and humility. The king should look into the affairs of the persons learned in the Vedas and of ascetics after going to the fire sanctuary and in the company of his chaplain and preceptor, after getting up from his seat and saluting those suitors.

In Indian culture, in the dealing with learned people like teachers and sanyasis, we have to take special care and profess love, respect and reverence. If there are any issues concerning these learned people, the king should not try to tackle them on his own. Even though the king has to take the important decisions regarding these respected groups of people, he is suggested to go to the fire sanctuary first.

Fire represents purity, and also sacrifice. The presence and blessings of fire purifies our mind and burns away the negativities. The Rig Veda, the first of the Vedas, starts with invoking fire (Agni): *Agnimeele purohitam yajnasya devam rtvijam, hotaram ratnadhatamam.* Meaning, I glorify Agni, the high priest of the sacrifice, the divine, the ministrant, who presents the oblation to the gods, and is the possessor of great wealth. Every ritual in the Vedic culture, like marriages or various yagnas, is conducted in the presence of the fire god, Agni.

After taking the blessings of fire, the king considers the matters of learned people and the ascetics in the company of his own chaplain (raja purohit) and preceptors (raja guru), so that he will be able to take their guidance in these sensitive matters.

Learned people are role models in our society and even if they are suitors, a person who makes a petition or request in the court of law, they have to be treated with great respect. Therefore, the king is advised to get up from his seat and offer his salutations first. This is our culture, where even the king has to show extreme humility before elders.

Thus, it is with the help of wise people that the king should consider their matters. He should decide the affairs of ascetics and of persons versed in the practice of magic in consultation with persons learned in the three Vedas, and not by himself, for the reason that they might be roused to anger.

We find an example in the story of Dusyanta, where this procedure is strictly followed when looking into the hermits' matter. If not, the hermits would have shown extreme anger and even cursed the kings.

Sunrise Time

Interestingly, the most important activities of the day are completed before the sun rises.

After meeting people of various types and considering their matters, the next one and half hours are spent with the heads of defence and the treasury. During the first eighth of the day, he should listen to the measures taken for defence and the accounts of income and expenditure.

The importance of the defence and the treasury in-charge (kosha-adhyaksha) is seen in various places in the *Arthashastra*. All undertakings are dependent first on the treasury; therefore, the king should look into the treasury first. The king brings under his sway his own party, as well as the party of the enemies, by the use of the treasury and the army. Even during emergencies, we find the king taking control of the army and treasury first. He should put the treasury and the army in one place, in the fortified city, in charge of trustworthy men.

Financial Matters

Leaders who take charge of the financial matters of the kingdom are better decision-makers and will be in control of the various issues and challenges that crop up on a regular basis. A sound economic structure can be created by building a strong treasury.

The treasury and the army are interconnected. Even among the saptanga these two are considered the important prakritis of a kingdom.

Thus, the regular monitoring of the two departments of finance and defence is allotted a large amount of focused time on a regular basis for review and immediate action.

Reflection of the Daily Routine of a King in the Panchamahakavyas

The dutiful rulers in the Panchamahakavyas were also aware of the fact that kingship was not only for their pleasure. To discharge their various duties successfully, the kings had to observe a strict daily timetable. From some scattered allusions and a mention of the daily programme of King Nala in 'Naisadacarita' (nineteenth canto), we can sketch out the daily routine of the kings in the Panchamahakavyas.

The king would be roused from the sleep by the auspicious eulogistic songs of the bards. These songs were called *bhogavali*, containing the description of the king's particular work at that time. Through these songs, the people would know about the tasks the king was occupied with. At dawn, the king finished the rites enjoined by the shastras and the morning ablutions.

Then he would visit the feudatory kings, who would touch his feet and offer marvellous jewels. In turn, he would ask them about their welfare.

Then, the valorous king would proceed to train students in the martial arts—in the use of weapons, in hurling and in striking.

He would then take a bath with fragrant paste and perfumed water.

After the bath, he would utter Vedic incantations while holding a crystal rosary. In the household temple, in the chamber of worship, he would pray to the gods with great devotion. Following the midday rites, the queen would join him for a meal.

The king would look into complicated conflicts that were brought before him and take prompt decisions, and also hold consultations with his ministers. After finishing his evening rites, in the second part of the night he would spend more time thinking about the administration of the kingdom. Consultations with spies also comprised a chief part of the king's daily timetable, though the exact time for it is not mentioned.

Rama, the Ideal King (Rajarishi)

Indian history has considered King Rama as the epitome of an ideal leader (*mariyada-purshottam*) and Ayodhya reflecting good governance (*rama rajya*). We find that even Rama followed this daily routine of a king with discipline.

In the seventeenth canto of 'Raghuvamsha', the poet himself states that whatever is ordained in the law books to be done by the rulers of the earth, in different divisions of the day and night, must be observed with a rigid resolve.

In this verse in 'Raghuvamsha' the words *niyoga* and *vikalpa* are purposefully approved, which are used by Kautilya to impress that work acquires success only by such a manner. In order to carry out his duties, the king was expected to be punctual and methodical, and he should not find any escape from his duties.

The king was expected to perform many other duties which are not mentioned in the daily programme of the king. In the course of his busy routine, he was expected to show himself to the subjects anxiously waiting him. The king was enjoined to make himself easily accessible to petitioners and to attend personally to their applications and complaints.

King Rama punctually attended to the affairs of the citizens, personally hearing every case of injustice. This personal contact with his subjects was an essential part of the king's daily routine.

Summary of the Daily Routine of a King

The daily routine of a king has its roots in early works, even before the *Arthashastra*. Kautilya refined these ancient ideas and reconstructed them for his generation. Thus, Kautilya was modern in his approach.

The general attitude of the king's daily programme reveals that it was influenced by the traditional model of a daily routine prescribed in the works on polity. For instance, Duryodhana, to reach the line of conduct laid down by

Manu, had allotted times for different functions in the days and the nights.

Flexible Timetable

This programme is not to be followed in a rigid manner by the kings. Kautilya himself mentions it as subject to modification, if necessary. But it also should be noted that kings definitely relied on this ideal timetable as their model.

We see that in the course of this model routine, a king has to multitask. There are times allotted for meetings with different people, administration, checks and supervision, revenue collection, entertainment, spiritual activities and also travel, all in one day. An alert king will be able to lead his people with dynamism. Therefore, the king should always be energetic.

However, Kautilya also allows the king the flexibility to decide and alter the routine as needed. Depending on the requirements of his situation, he could choose what he should do. A king should divide the day and night into different parts in conformity with his capacity and carry out his tasks.

Every person has different times and energy levels at which they are able to be productive and effective. Additionally, each person's capacity is different. All this and more should be taken into consideration while preparing a king's timetable.

There is a difference between clarity and rigidity. It is with clear thinking that the routine planned, not with rigidity. Thus, being ever active, the king should carry out the management of material and spiritual well-being.

A king is made to understand his duties clearly. Thus he is bound to serve better. And Chanakya ensured that through aanvikshiki.

9

Human and Divine Thinking

The world is not just what we see and feel. There are many worlds that exist simultaneously. Few people understand this and can operate in multiple worlds.

The world that we live in includes the people, the objects and emotions. Most of us believe that is the real world. However, spiritual masters can feel and understand other worlds too: The world of the spirit. The world of divinity. The world of gods and other divine beings.

All these multiple worlds are interconnected. And we all live in these worlds without being aware of it. From time to time, we get a glimpse of it in our dreams or during our prayers. As this world is real, so too, those other worlds are also real.

Chanakya understood this. And he also knew that if we want to succeed in this world, we need to take help from the beings in the other worlds too. Many people try to do this through pujas, yajnas, rituals, prayers, sacrifices, penance and prayers.

In the *Arthashastra*, we find that Chanakya knew about the existence of the other worlds, and used many of his strategies to connect to the other worlds as well.

Human thinking has limitations. Divine thinking, though, is limitless. Once we are able to combine human thinking with divine thinking—we can operate in a completely different way. We combine the world of sense and the world beyond senses. We will be aided and guided by people from other worlds as well as people in this world.

Chanakya was an extremely intelligent human being. His was probably one of the most brilliant intellects that the human race has ever seen. But what made him so was using help from other worlds as well.

In this chapter we will see two aspects.

1. How to use human thinking (with the help of experts)
2. How to use divine thinking (through the invocation of the world of spirits)

The combination of both is what goes inside the mind of Chanakya.

But remember—it is the results that finally matter.

1. How to Use Human Thinking (With the Help of Experts)

According to Chanakya, a person should never think alone. What can one brain alone do? Make use of the brains of others as well to achieve your goals. Additionally, one person can only think of certain possibilities. By including the thinking of others, you can expand your horizons to include a multitude of possibilities.

This is the process of brainstorming. One plus one is greater than two. This is the concept of synergy. When two minds come together, they can see a third possibility. Why think alone when there are many to help you?

But we should also be careful in selecting others we are going to use. Make sure you have better minds to guide you. Thus Chanakya's concept of associating with elders to get good guidance comes into play.

Association with Elders

Vriddhasnyoga—being in association with one's elders. This is learning from real-life experts from various fields to improve leadership, management and financial skills. The journey to meet and learn from real-life experts should go on forever.

There are three types of people: those who don't learn from their mistakes; those who learn from their mistakes; and the best, those who learn from others' mistakes as well as their own. 'Association with elders' means learning from those who are more mature and experienced than you. To always keep learning is one of the qualities of a great leader.

Advice from Amatyas (Ministers)

Amatyas or ministers are the king's advisers and councillors.

The ministers are the second-in-charge of a kingdom. The country depends on the ministers for decisions when the leader is not around. In the *Arthashastra*, the importance of a minister is emphasized repeatedly. In fact, chapter eight of book one is titled *amatya-utpatti*, meaning 'appointment of ministers'.

Who is an amatya? He can be called a mantri or a minister. There are many people in the government who play the role of amatyas. The cabinet secretary is an amatya for the chief minister, while the national security adviser is an important amatya for the prime minister.

As Chanakya points out:

> Rulership can be successfully carried out only with the help
> of associates. One wheel alone does not turn. Therefore,
> he (the ruler) should appoint ministers and listen to their
> opinion. (1.7.9)

Let us delve deeper into this verse.

The help of associates: A king has to manage a large kingdom, which is impossible to do alone. Those who think that they can do everything on their own will never grow. Leaders know the importance of teamwork. In the olden days, the king had associates in the form of his friends, teachers, mentors and gurus. These are his strong associates.

One wheel alone does not turn: The king cannot run a kingdom alone. He requires amatyas along with him. Kautilya gives an analogy here. If there is only one wheel in a bullock cart, the cart keeps going in circles. There is movement but no progress. There is action but no direction. Vehicles that have to carry heavy cargo and lots of people have many wheels. The bigger the vehicle, the more the wheels required and the stronger they should be. Big trucks sometimes have forty or fifty wheels to transport heavy machinery. So in larger countries like ours, we have various cabinet ministers to manage different departments.

Advice on strong financials: The *Arthashastra* talks about a strong treasury, or kosha, which keeps the kingdom going. Kautilya says that the primary task of the king is to focus on the acquisition, growth and expansion of the treasury. A strong and well-managed treasury should also be secured and protected.

The *Arthashastra* suggests that a king should have a sound understanding of economics; it among the first subjects he learns in the educational system (vaarta). In the daily timetable of a king, the first activity should be checking the accounts of the kingdom. The kosha-adhyaksha, or the finance head, must bring in daily reports and inform the king about the kingdom's financial situation. The king cannot lose track of the nation's finances and should have complete control over it. When the treasury is having problems, he should take immediate measures to fill it up.

Artha is wealth and shastra is scripture. Therefore, the *Arthashastra* itself means a scripture of wealth. Scholars have called it a book of economics that covers everything from microeconomics to macroeconomics, accounting systems to auditing rules, the collection of taxes and fines to the utilization of public funds for the development of a kingdom.

It often believed that since Indians are spiritual in nature, they do not understand wealth and material possessions very well. This is not true. We know the practical value of wealth and money. We also know its limitations and problems that arise out of greed. We were one of the most prosperous nations in the world at one point. Not to mention that Indians evolved a theory of economics that the Western world has yet to grasp.

The *Arthashastra* is proof of this. It is a book on the knowledge of wealth and is a wealth of knowledge. A study of the *Arthashastra* helps us to understand our past in its full glory, and the principles of wealth described in the *Arthashastra* can be directly applied to our generation and can be a tool of financial application in various situations.

Whether in the past or in the present, finance is the backbone of any undertaking. Every individual, family, society, organization, institution or nation is dependent on money and finances. A strong and well-managed treasury is the heart of any organization.

Taking the treasury as the basis, various governments create their national and state budgets. Good economic policies create employment and an atmosphere conducive to the growth of trade, business and entrepreneurship. Thus, sound control and management of the treasury leads to the prosperity of the king, the citizens and the kingdom.

From a philosophical standpoint, it is important to understand wealth and money. A responsible leader will never underestimate the value of money. A leader, however, has to be 'money-conscious' and not 'money-minded'.

A money-conscious leader understands money and gives it the right place and value. A money-minded leader, however, views the world only from a financial perspective. His attitude is, 'What is in it for me?' He is corrupt and selfish.

Great leaders work on finances, but understand that the vision of any project is more important than the finance itself.

These leaders are industrious; they are risk-takers; they work for the benefit of the society, to create wealth for everyone. They are the leaders who create positive change.

The *Arthashastra* details a financial model called 'The Four Stages of Wealth', which can be applied for a nation. The four stages are:

1. Wealth identification
2. Wealth creation
3. Wealth management
4. Wealth distribution

Wealth identification: The identification of wealth is the starting point. What is the real wealth of our nation? Talented people, our culture, our industrious spirit—all these are our national wealth. If we are able to put them into the right use, we can become the wealthiest nation in the world. From a situation of brain drain, we can move to brain gain.

Wealth creation: Creating wealth is hard work. It is a laborious task that requires patience and a long-term approach. But with hard work and the help of experts, we can succeed. People only see the success but not the struggling days of discipline, consistency and patience. Wealth creation for a nation can happen when everyone participates in the process. Each person in the country has to work ethically and selflessly.

Wealth management: Once you have overcome the challenge of creating wealth, the next step is to manage it. The problem is that the level of wealth created has to be maintained.

We have seen that some people who suddenly become wealthy lose everything just as quickly. So we need to know how to conserve our wealth and invest it for the future. A leader knows that days ahead may not be as good as today. So save for the rainy days.

Wealth distribution: The wealth created by the country has to go back to its people. Distribute it to the less privileged. Today, companies also do this in various ways, like through CSR (corporate social responsibility) activities. The cycle of wealth cannot be complete till it is given back to the society from where it comes.

If these four stages are managed properly, wealth will give us great and lasting happiness.

Advice from Friends

The seventh element of a state is mitra—the ally or the friend.

A mitra is a friend, philosopher and guide, one who is always with you through the good and bad times. A friend in need is a friend indeed. He also acts like a mentor and sounding board from time to time. Having good allies is vital for the king.

Even the most powerful king will require a mitra. He can hold a mirror and show you what is real. He is the lighthouse that shows you the way. He is the consultant who offers you the right advice at the right time.

The story of the Mahabharata illustrates the importance of choosing the right mitra. Before the war of Kurukshetra, both the Pandavas and Kauravas sought the support of various kings. Both parties wanted help from Krishna. When approached, Krishna wanted to support both his cousins. He decided to split himself into two, as it were—his army on one side and Krishna as an unarmed charioteer on the other side. Arjuna chose the company of Krishna, while Duryodhana was happy getting his powerful army.

This made all the difference in the war. The Pandavas won the war due to Krishna's strategic advice at every turn. As Arjuna's charioteer, Krishna was always with them, guiding them towards success.

Such is the power of choosing the right advisers. An intelligent person is the biggest asset of any team or organization. Successful companies understand the value of good advisers. Therefore, they have advisory panels that guide them from time to time. So, when the going gets tough, take the help of mitras.

Some people hesitate or feel belittled if they have to ask for help. This is a disaster. No one is perfect. Therefore, asking a friend for help can save a lot of trouble. Make use of friends and let friends use you. Friendship is always a win-win situation for both parties.

A good leader is open-minded and ready to work with alliances. He is surrounded by people who are better than him in various fields. In book one, chapter fifteen, verses thirty-five and forty of the *Arthashastra*, Kautilya says:

All undertakings should be preceded by consultations. Holding a consultation with only one, he may not be able to reach a decision in difficult matters. With more councillors, it is difficult to reach decisions and maintain secrecy.

A king is as good or bad as his advisers. Therefore, the leader has to be selective in his choice of advisers and the advice he gets, because the decisions he takes based on the advice can make or break a nation or kingdom.

All undertakings: The important word is 'all'. The leader should always consult others before any and all activities, big or small. Thus, he will think along with others and not just in isolation. Multiple minds will be working together, even before the undertaking begins.

Holding a consultation with only one: Kautilya gives a warning to the leader here. Having a single adviser will make you too dependent on that person. He may guide you, but there is also the danger that he may misguide you. Take a second opinion.

Mature in intellect: It is very important for an adviser to be intellectually mature. The adviser may be young, yet mature and an expert in that particular field. This is often seen in the police force, in the case of cybercrime. The experts are generally young police officers. They understand the technical issues better than the most senior officers.

Sit and counsel: Sitting here is symbolic. The term *Upanishad* means sitting below a spiritual master and listening to his wisdom. Similarly, when one is sitting with a mature and intelligent person, one should be receptive like a good student in the class. Not just listening, but also discussing the problem and asking him questions to obtain clarity on the issues concerned.

Thus, using the varied advice given by various people, Chanakya makes the king strong in his thinking and decision-making processes.

Now, after making use of human thinking, Chanakya advises the king to take divine thinking into account.

2. How to Use Divine Thinking (Through Invoking the World of Spirits)

Many believe that taking into consideration the world of spirits is very unpractical. However, according to Chanakya, it is a very practical thing to do. It is not blind faith that we should adopt, but the understanding that there are factors beyond human control.

So when a problem arises, we try various solutions. Either with the help of advisers or through alternative methods. But often, we still will not get the results that we want. And then, we try the divine methods.

As a joke about alternative medical treatments goes, 'When allopathy does not work, we try homeopathy. And when that also does not work, finally Tirupati.'

Chanakya considers these aspects in his thinking.

In book eight, chapter one, verse two of the *Arthashastra*, Chanakya says:

> A calamity of a constituent, of a divine or human origin,
> springs from ill luck or wrong policy.

Assume there is a fire in a place, and in spite of the fire protection systems, about fifty people die—who will be held responsible? One could say it was due to bad luck. Despite a strong fire policy, fifty people could not escape the fire. Chanakya here factors in ill luck also.

In life, in spite of the best planning, things can go wrong. The best of satellite launches can fail. In the final match, the best team can lose to an easy opponent. But the fire at the Mantralaya of Maharashtra on 21 June 2012 demonstrated how ill prepared the building was for such a disaster.

Therefore, one cannot blame bad luck if efforts were not taken to avoid it and proper planning was not in place. One cannot go to the examination hall without preparation, expecting good luck to pass you. As leaders, we need to understand that right policies are about lots of planning and effort.

One has to prepare for surprises well in advance. In the planning of the durga too, all possible types of enemy attacks were planned for and factored into the building of the fort.

In today's world, infrastructure is both physical and digital. In the workplace, apart from good offices, digital infrastructure, which includes computers, Internet connectivity and mobile phones, is equally important. The leaders of today's nations should plan for airports, roads, housing, transportation systems and marketplaces for their people.

While constructing these, we should consider the divine aspects too. Therefore, the traditional practice in India is to perform a puja and invoke divine blessings before starting any work. Lord Ganesha is invoked as a *vighnaharta*—the one who removes all obstacles (human and divine) on the path towards success.

We find Chanakya also using these divine and even occult practices with fighting with the enemy. He says:

> Practices accompanied by mantras and medicines and those that are caused by illusion—with them he should destroy the enemies and protect his own people. (14.3.88)

There are many war rituals given in the *Arthashastra*. These mantras are used to destroy the enemy. Even in the modern days, there are pandits and priests on the payroll of the army. Their role is to invoke the blessings of the divine before and during the war.

Chanakya also uses various types of medicines to treat his injured soldiers. Some of these medicines are also divine in nature, created by invoking certain mantras. In our Ayurvedic literature, we find mention of such medicines, and also how to prepare these medicines or find them.

One example is the Sanjeevani herb that is mentioned in the Ramayana. When Lakshmana was facing death, Hanuman went and got the herb to save his life. This kind of medicine, given at the right time, can save lives of the whole group.

Finally, Results Matter

We may use human thinking and also divine thinking. But finally, it is the results that matter. Chanakya was a result-focused person. Try this way or that way—we should achieve success.

Therefore, to practise aanvikshiki, he also gives us some methods. The definition of effective deliberation (thinking) is given in book one, chapter fifteen of verse forty-two in the *Arthashastra*,

> The means of starting undertakings, the excellence of men and material, (suitable) apportionment of place and time, provision against failure (and) accomplishment of work—this is deliberation (reflection) in its five aspects.

In this one line, Kautilya defines the five principles of sound thinking. These are skills that an amatya needs to possess or develop. All theories and concepts are based on certain principles.

Let us take a look at these five principles of right thinking defined by Kautilya.

The means of starting undertakings: A good minister, like a good king, also takes initiatives and starts new projects. For instance, the railway minister (an amatya to the prime minister) would start new projects like introducing new railway routes, computerized systems and so on.

Steven Covey, in his book, *The Seven Habits of Highly Effective People*, describes this as being proactive. This is an important quality of a good swami and a good amatya too.

Excellence of men and materials: An amatya has access to lots of resources. These resources include funds, his team of people and even infrastructure. How to utilize them fully and effectively is the challenge of the amatya.

Shivaji as a leader had Tanaji and other amatyas with him. They in turn were the senapatis and led the soldiers to fight effectively.

Suitable place and time: Right thinking (aanvikshiki) is about deciding the right place and time to make your move. In warfare, for instance, timing is very crucial. When to attack the enemy is not an easy question to answer. It requires careful planning, analysis and also patience. This sense of the right timing comes from one's own experience and knowledge and guidance from other sources.

Field Marshal Manekshaw was an exceptional strategist. Under his command, Indian forces conducted victorious campaigns against Pakistan in the war of 1971 that led to the liberation of Bangladesh in December 1971. His sense of timing on the battlefield was admired by one and all, and was one of the qualities that led to his success.

Provision against failure: Every move has to be planned taking two alternatives into consideration; the best-case scenario of complete success and the worst-case scenario of total failure. A back-up plan is required for each move. One needs to be prepared with alternative solutions in case of failures.

A leader was once asked the reason for his success, to which he replied, 'I take into consideration failures at each stage. I plan alternative moves even before I start a venture.'

Accomplishment of work: Finally, leadership is about achieving results. It is very important to have parameters to check whether you have achieved what you set out to do. Every project is started with a certain objective in mind. The process may evolve as the project is executed, but finally, the goal has to be achieved, even if the route taken is different from what was initially planned.

One of the main duties of the Comptroller and Auditor General of India is not only to perform financial audits but also 'performance audits'. Every government institution, such as universities and research institutions (the Defence Research and Development Organization or the Bhabha Atomic Research Centre, among others), has parameters on which its results are evaluated. Based on these performances, their productivity is measured.

India as a nation has gone through various changes in its political scene. During the times of Chanakya the form of governance was monarchy, while today it is a democracy, with elected governments. However, some wonder if democracy is the best form of governance.

Some thinkers have also asked, if democracy is not the best form of governance, which is the better alternative? We have seen that monarchy by itself did not lead to good governance. Some monarchs also became dictators and tyrants. If the whole world is moving towards democracy as a good model of governance, then is there a better version of democracy than the existing form?

These questions were considered, debated and discussed by this research scholar internally and externally with various experts. And in that search for a better model of 'good governance', it was important to study the various aspects of Kautilian thoughts. The *Arthashastra* explores governance, from the various dimensions of a leader to his philosophy on how to govern. Therefore, in this research we have explored various unknown philosophical dimensions of leadership.

One clear observation was that finally, any form of governance depends on the king/leader who is the head of the kingdom or the state. So clearly, Kautilya indicated that creating a good leader, who in turn has an able team of able ministers running the government machinery, provides good governance for its people.

Chanakya taught aanvikshiki, also called philosophy and the right way of thinking. In challenging situations, how the king can apply aanvikshiki was understood in this book.

We also dealt with Kautilya's 'rajarishi'—an ideal leader. The *Arthashastra* does not just explore what a king should do, but also twenty-one things to be avoided by the king. But to become a rajarishi, it is important to understand the concept of dharma, which is the very essence of Indian philosophy.

If everyone in society is clear about his/her role, there will be harmony and peace. The rajarishi operates out of the understanding of dharma from all these aspects.

We also understood the saptanga leadership model of a kingdom. The seven pillars of a kingdom—swami, amatya, janapada, durga, kosha, danda and mitra—and what the *Arthashastra* says about their ideal qualities were seen. The saptanga model has been tested by this research scholar with various leaders, organizations and institutions. We looked at the successful application of each *anga* in our modern days.

One should not be happy just by finding something after years of research. One should make sure society benefits from the discoveries. The best way to do this was to spread the knowledge of leadership to as many people as possible.

Ideas on how to build and contribute to the pool of knowledge of the *Arthashastra* were included in this book. One should study the full *Arthashastra* (6000 sutras) of Kautilya under the guidance of a good teacher to understand these concepts better.

With the blessings of other scholars and teachers, one can contribute in a very significant and relevant manner to the field of knowledge. We can reconstruct the wisdom of the *Arthashastra* for our generation.

As Swami Chinmayananda put it, 'What you have is God's gift to you, what you do with what you have is your gift to God.' Similarly, we have the wisdom of the *Arthashastra* with us, and what we do with that wisdom will be our gift to him. Let us aim at creating ideal leaders—rajarishis in our generation.

The leadership ideas given in Kautilya's *Arthashastra* has contemporary relevance. These ideas when applied by a leader will result in extremely efficient government machinery and happy citizens. It can also be applied by people who are not leaders by position in order to develop leadership qualities. Thus, one day it will naturally lead them to leadership positions in their respective fields. Good leaders create good societies.

Thus, it can be concluded that the leadership ideas given by Chanakya in the *Arthashastra* is a living force and relevant in modern times and for the future. The research findings and philosophy have to be applied in the real world.

The urgent need for good, ethical and philosophical leaders for our nation, society and the world at large can be fulfilled through these research findings.

A rajarishi, along with the dharmic praja following their respective duties, creates an ideal spiritual society—the ultimate aim of any model of 'good governance'. This is the main work and objective of aanvikshiki—the science of thinking.

10

Inside Your Mind

As we come to the end of this book, let us revisit its objective. The central idea of this book is to bring to you the concept of aanvikshiki, which is almost lost to our generation. However, through this book we have also tried to go 'inside Chanakya's mind'.

But by now we are certain that Chanakya has entered our minds as well. Allow him to enter your thoughts—and he will transform you completely. You will be a totally changed person—you will be reborn.

So the ultimate objective of the book is to use the principles of aanvikshiki and also to bring out the 'Chanakya in you'.

In this concluding chapter, let us talk about your understanding of Chanakya and of aanvikshiki. This will be an exercise for you to do in your minds and see how you think differently. I will be asking you a few questions and you need to give answers from your study of this book and the life of Chanakya. I will also give you some tips and sutras of Chanakya to help you think the Chanakya way.

Practise this method of thinking in your life on a regular basis. Inside your mind, you will see Chanakya guiding you. And remember . . . Chanakya never fails.

1. What according to you is aanvikshiki?

Tip: We have studied how Kautilya's *Arthashastra* defines aanvikshiki in the first chapter.

Guiding sutra:

> Aanvikshiki is ever thought of as the lamp of all sciences, as the means of all actions and as the support of all laws and duties. (1.2.12)

Your notes:

....

....

....

....

....

....

....

....

....

....

....

....

2. What is the saptanga model of the *Arthashastra*?

Tip: It is included in chapter four, 'The Seven Dimensions of Thinking'.

Guiding sutra:

> Swami, amatya, janapada, durga, kosha, dand, mitra—iti prakritaya. (6.1.1)
> The king, the minister, the country (people), the fortified city, the treasury, the army and the ally—are the constituent elements (of the kingdom). (6.1.1)

Your notes:

....
....
....
....
....
....
....
....
....
....
....
....
....

3. What is the importance of a shatru (enemy), according to Chanakya?

Tip: It is included in chapter five, 'The Eighth Dimension of Thinking'.

Guiding sutra:

> Excluding the enemy, these seven constituent elements
> have been described with each one's excellences manifest;
> those, when they operate, become subordinate to the
> excellences of the king. (6.1.15)

Your notes:

....

....

....

....

....

....

....

....

....

....

....

....

....

4. What are the guiding principles of leadership and management as given in the *Arthashastra*?

Tip: It is included in chapter seven, 'Chanakya's Thoughts on Management'.

Guiding sutra:

> Prajasukhe Sukham Raja, Prajacha Hite Hitam . . . (1.19.34)
> In the happiness of the subjects lies the benefit of the king and in what is beneficial to the subjects is his own benefit. (1.19.34)

Your notes:

....

....

....

....

....

....

....

....

....

....

....

....

....

5. What are your views on Chanakya being a cunning and shrewd person?

Tip: It is included in chapter six, 'The Other Side of Chanakya'.

Guiding sutra:

> He should establish contacts with forest chieftains, frontier-chiefs and chief officials in the cities and the countryside. (1.16.7)

Your notes:

....

....

....

....

....

....

....

....

....

....

....

....

....

....

6. How many hours is a king (leader) supposed to sleep in day?

Tip: It is included in chapter six, 'The Other Side of Chanakya'.

Guiding sutra:

> A shadow measuring three paurusas, one paurusa (and) four angulas, and the midday when the shadow disappears, these are the four earlier eighth part of the day. Similarly are explained the later four parts. (1.19)

Your notes:

....

....

....

....

....

....

....

....

....

....

....

....

....

....

....

....

7. How to take advice from others?

Tip: It is included in chapter nine, 'Human Thinking and Divine Thinking'.

Guiding sutra:

> Rulership can be successfully carried out only with the help of associates. One wheel alone does not turn. Therefore, he (the ruler) should appoint ministers and listen to their opinion. (1.7.9)

Your notes:

....

....

....

....

....

....

....

....

....

....

....

....

....

....

8. How to take divine help in solving problems?

Tip: It is included in chapter nine, 'Human Thinking and Divine Thinking'.

Guiding sutra:

> A calamity of a constituent, of a divine or human origin, springs from ill luck or wrong policy. (8.1.2)

Your notes:

....

....

....

....

....

....

....

....

....

....

....

....

....

....

....

9. What are the different models of thinking in this book?

Tip: It is included in chapter nine, 'Different Models of Thinking'.

Guiding sutra:

> From the capacity for doing work is the ability of a person judged. And in accordance with their ability, by suitably distributing rank among ministers and assigning the place, time and work (to them), he should appoint these ministers. (1.8.28–29)

Your notes:

....

....

....

....

....

....

....

....

....

....

....

....

....

10. What will you do whenever you are faced with a problem henceforth?

Tip: This whole book is a guide for you.

Guiding sutra:

> No guidance from anyone . . .
> You are now your own Chanakya . . .

Your notes:

....

....

....

....

....

....

....

....

....

....

....

....

....

....

....

Acknowledgements

This book would not have happened without one person: Milee Ashwarya.

When the discussion about writing a book began with Penguin Random House almost three years ago, the first answer was not so positive from my side due to my hectic schedules. But Milee's patience and persistence finally made this book happen. Thank you, Milee.

Thanks to the whole team at Penguin Random House for their efforts.

The topic of my book is very close to my heart as Aanvikshiki is the name of my daughter. This is a new word for most of us. When I found this word (and the science of thinking in the *Arthashastra*), I was thrilled. I could not resist naming my daughter Aanvikshiki. Not everyone liked this unique name, but my family members let me have my way. My parents, C.K.K. and Sushila Pillai, my parents-in-law, Shekar and Dhanavathi Shetty, my sister-in-laws, Chandrika and Sarikha, (and Sarikha's husband, Ajay)—thanks to all of you and my friends as I listen to the sound of the word again and again every day when you call her name.

My sincere thanks to my teachers Dr Shubhada Joshi and Dr Gangdharan Nair who helped my research and PhD on the *Arthashastra* become a part of my daily thinking. And to Swami Tejomayananda and Swami Advayananda of the Chinmaya Mission, who helped me to study and understand aanvikshiki in its deep roots of spirituality.